N° 45

MAP

BRU

GIRAULT GILBERT

A Division of GEOCART s.p.r.l.

Publisher & Copyright Cartography : GIRAULT GILBERT,
a division of Geocart s.p.r.l., rue d'Ophem 64
B-1000 Bruxelles

D/9704/3020/019 - ISBN 90-6736-184-4

INSTRUCTIONS FOR USE

The map is divided into 192 squares, each one representing 470 meters.

To find the whereabouts of a street, refer to the street index. The name of the street is followed by the name of the Parish Council, and finally by a letter and number which represents the square in which you will find the street you are looking for.

Example : rue Baron Horta
See : Horta (rue Baron) B- J6
Abbreviation : H.P. signifies outside plan limit

SUMMARY

PARISH COUNCILS, ABBREVIATIONS .... Page 2, 38
PUBLIC TRANSPORT 3
Underground - Trams and buses of Brussels (S.T.I.B) - Main stations - Foreign Railways - Airline companies - Steamship lines.
TOURIST INFORMATION 11
Addresses - Hotels - Youth hostels - Restaurants - Architecture art nouveau - Markets - Shopping - Yearly Events
VARIOUS INFORMATION 13
European organizations - Permanent representations - Post offices - Gendarmerie - Police - Religions - Embassies - Consulates - Parkings.
SPORTS 18
Parks and gardens - Stadiums - Football - Rugby - Hockey - Tennis - Indoor swimming pools - Skating - Bowling - Camping sites - Golf courses.
SPECTACLES 19
Stages and entertainments - Cultural Centre - Cinemas
BRUPARC 21
GRAND-PLACE 22
PRINCIPAL MONUMENTS AND SIGHTS 27
PRINCIPAL MUSEUMS 34
INDEX TO STREETS 38

PARISH COUNCILS, ABBREVIATIONS

ANDERLECHT	An
AUDERGHEM	Au
BERCHEM -STE-AGATHE	BA
BRUXELLES	B
ETTERBEEK	Et
EVERE	Ev
FOREST	Fo
GANSHOREN	Ga
IXELLES	XL
JETTE	JP
KOEKELBERG	Ko
MOLENBEEK-ST-JEAN	Mo
ST-GILLES	SG
ST-JOSSE-TEN-NODE	SJ
SCHAERBEEK	Sc
WOLUWE-ST-LAMBERT	WL
WOLUWE-ST-PIERRE	WP

Metro - Premetro

Métro - Pré-métro

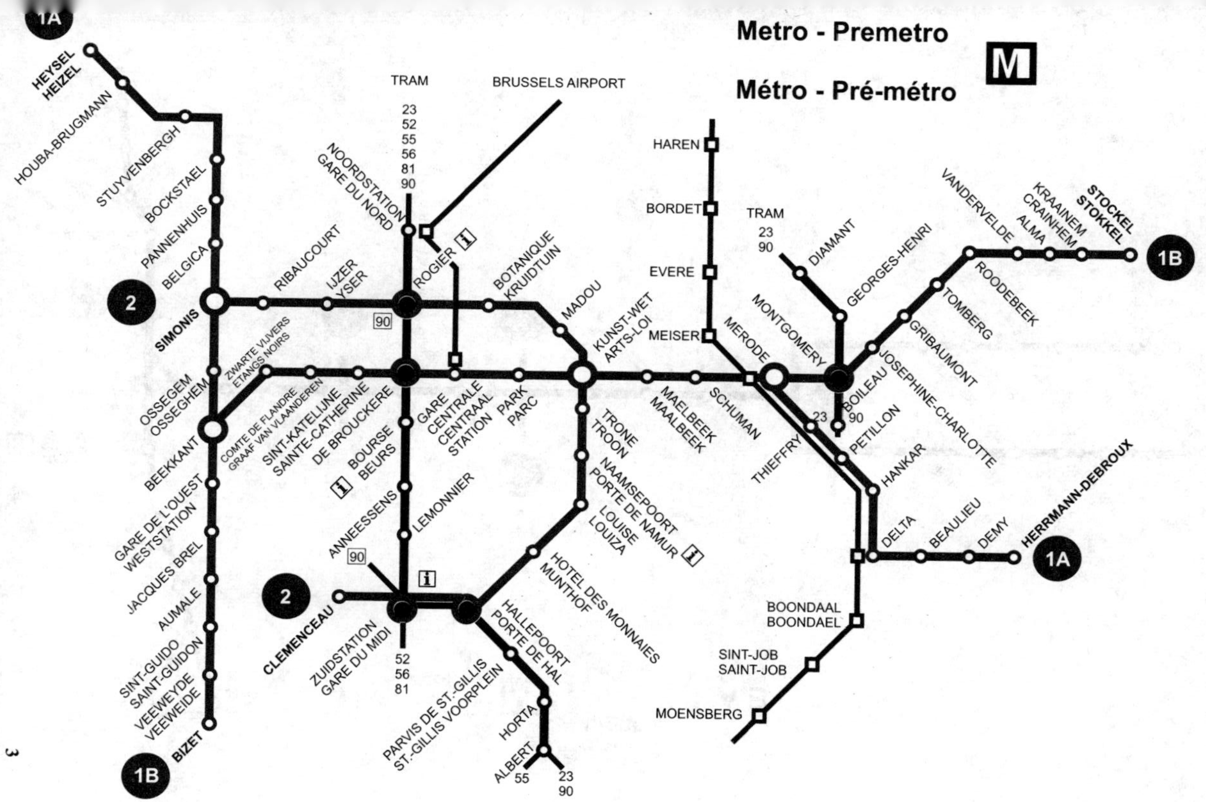

Ligne / Lijn 1 A B

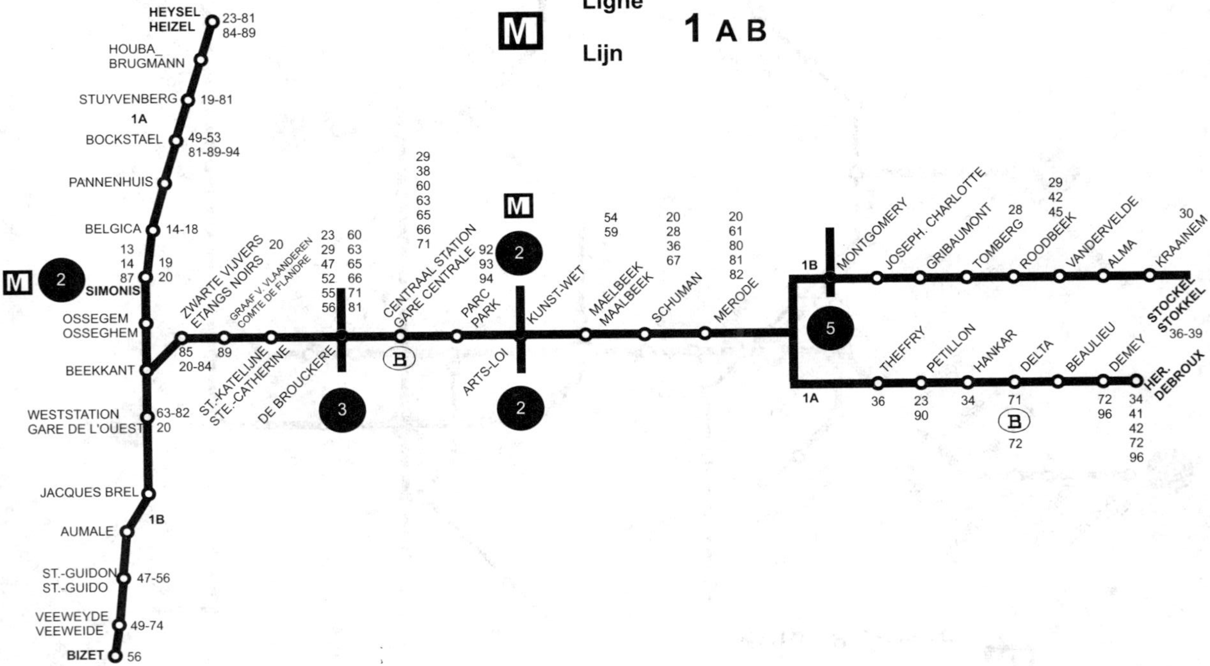

M Ligne 2 Lijn

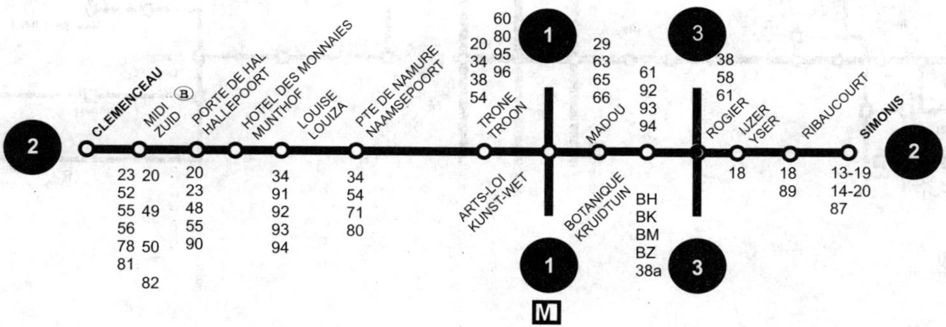

Pré - métro Ligne

Premetro Lijn

3 : 23 - 52 - 55 - 56 - 81

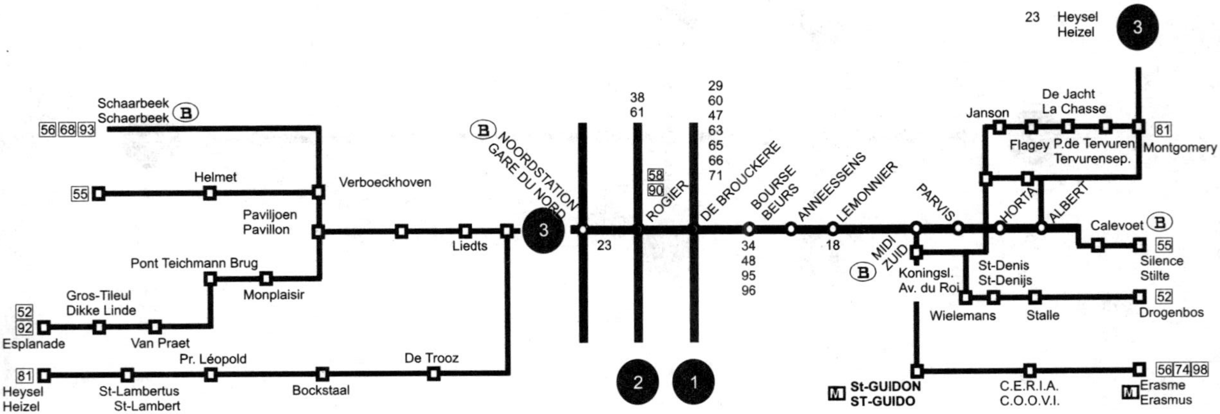

Pré - métro Ligne / Pré- metro Lijn **5 : 23 - 90**

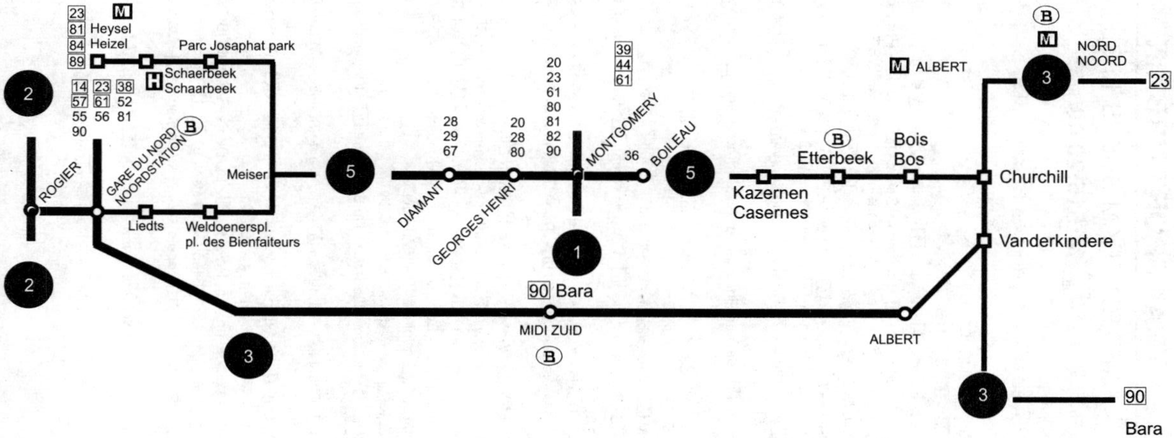

TRANSPORT URBAIN

METRO TRAM BUS (S.T.I.B.)

[i] ☎ 515.20.00

1A [M] HEYSEL - HERRMANN-DEBROUX

1B [M] BIZET - STOCKEL

2 [M] SIMONIS - CLEMENCEAU

13 SIMONIS [M] - [H] A.Z. V.U.B.

14 NORD (B) [M] - Belgica [M] - Simonis [M] - Miroir - [H] A.Z. V.U.B.

18 HOUBA DE STROOPER - [H] Brugmann - Belgica [M] - Yser [M] - Porte de Flandre - Midi (B) [M] - Barr. de St.-Gilles - Wielemans - St.-Denis - DIEWEG

19 GROOT-BIJGAARDEN - Basilique - Simonis [M] - "DE WAND"

20 HUNDERENVELD - Simonis [M] - Etangs Noirs [M] - Midi (B) [M] - Pl. Royale - Trône [M] - Q. Léopold (B) - Montgomery [M] - VERHEYLEWEGHEN

23 HEYSEL [M] - Pr. Elisabeth - Meiser - Montgomery [M] - Bois - Albert-Midi (B) [M] - GARE DU NORD (B) [M]

28 SCHUMAN (B) [M] - de Jamblinne de Meux - Georges-Henri [M] - Tomberg [M] - STADE FALLON

29 DE BROUCKERE [M] - Gare Centrale (B) [M] - Madou [M] - Plasky - Verheyleweghen - HOF-TEN-BERG

30 CRAINHEM [M] - Wezembeek - OPPEM

34 BOURSE [M] - Sablon - Louise [M] - Porte de Namur [M] - La Chasse - Hankar [M] - TRANSVAAL

36 SCHUMAN (B) [M] - La Chasse - Chant d'Oiseau - Woluwe - Ste-Alix - STOCKEL [M]

38 NORD (B) [M] - Gare Centrale (B) [M] - Trône [M] - Flagey - Danco - Calevoet (B) - HOMBORCH

39 MONTGOMERY [M] - Woluwe - Stockel [M] - BAN EIK

41 CALEVOET (B) - Marlow - [H] Ste Elisabeth - Keym - Wiener - HERRMANN-DEBROUX [M]

42 WIENER - Herrmann-Debroux [M] - Woluwe - Roodebeek [M] - [H] UCL St.-Luc - VIADUC E40

43 HEROS - Calevoet (B) - Bourdon Linkebeek (B) - Homborch - VIVIER D'OIE

44 MONTGOMERY [M] - Woluwe - TERVUREN

45 ROODEBEEK [M] - de Paduwa - ST.VINCENT

47 VILVOORDE - [H] Militaire - De Trooz - De Brouckère [M] - Clemenceau [M] - St.Guidon [M] - MOORTEBEEK

48 BOURSE [M] - Chapelle - Pte de Hal [M] - Barrière de St.-Gilles - Albert [M] - Altitude Cent - UCCLE-STALLE (B)

49 BOCKSTAEL (B) [M] - Basilique - Mettewie - Saint-Guidon [M] - Wielemans - MIDI (B) [M]

50 MIDI (B) [M] - St.Denis - Ruisbroek - LOT

52 ESPLANADE - Verboekhoven - Nord (B) [M] - St.-Denis - DROGENBOS

53 VAL MARIA - P. Benoit - Gros Tilleul - Bockstael (B) [M] - [H] Brugmann - [H] A.Z.V.U.B.

54 MACHELEN - St.-Vincent - Q. Léopold (B) - Porte de Namur [M] - Ma Campagne - Albert [M] - ST.-DENIS

55 BORDET (B) - Pl. Paix - Verboekhoven - Nord (B) [M] - Midi (B) [M] - Albert [M] - Calevoet (B) - SILENCE

56 SCHAERBEEK (B) - Verboekhoven - Nord (B) [M] - Midi (B) [M] - St.-Guidon [M] - C.E.R.I.A. - [H] ERASME

57 [H] MILITAIRE - Van Praet - De Trooz - NORD(B) [M]

58 VILVOORDE - Buda - Schaerbeek(B) - ROGIER [M]

59 BORDET(B) - Schaerbeek(B) - St.-Josse - Maelbeek [M] - Jourdan - Flagey - [H] ETTERBEEK-IXELLES

60 DE BROUCKERE [M] - Gare Centrale(B) [M] - Trône [M] - Flagey - G. Brugmann - Observatoire - VIVIER D'OIE

61 NORD(B) [M] - Botanique [M] - Dailly - MONTGOMERY [M]

63 MAES - Cimetière Bruxelles - Plasky - Madou [M] - De Brouckère [M] - Gare de l'Ouest [M] - MACHTENS

65 N.A.T.O - Chazal - Bienfaiteurs - Madou [M] - Gare Centrale(B) [M] - DE BROUCKERE [M]

66 CIMETIERE BRUXELLES - de Paduwa - Madou [M] - Gare Centrale(B) [M] - DE BROUCKERE [M]

67 BORDET(B) - Cimetière Bruxelles - de Paduwa - Diamant [M] - SCHUMAN(B) [M]

68 J. BORDET - Bordet(B) - SCHAERBEEK(B)

71 DE BROUCKERE [M] - Gare Centrale(B) [M] - Porte de Namur [M] - Flagey - U.L.B. - DELTA [M]

72 U.L.B. - H. Debroux [M] - A.D.E.P.S.

74 VEEWEYDE [M] - [H] ERASME

78 MIDI(B) [M] - Petite Ile - HUMANITE

80 ANDROMEDE - Georges-Henri [M] - Montgomery [M] - Jourdan - PORTE DE NAMUR [M]

81 HEYSEL [M] - Bockstael(B) [M] - Nord(B) [M] - Midi(B) [M] - Bar. de St.-Gilles - La Chasse - MONTGOMERY [M]

82 BERCHEM(B) - Gare de l'Ouest [M] - Midi(B) [M] - Barrière St.-Gilles - La Chasse - MONTGOMERY [M]

84 BEEKKANT [M] - Elbers - Berchem(B) - [H] A.Z.V.U.B. - Cité Modèle - HEYSEL [M]

85 BEEKKANT [M] - Schweitzer - BERCHEM(B)

87 SIMONIS [M] - Basilique - BASILIX

89 HEYSEL [M] - [H] Brugmann - Bockstael(B) [M] - Comte de Flandre [M] - Jacques Brel [M] - Peterbos - WESTLAND SHOPPING

90 ROGIER [M] - Liedts - Bienfaiteurs - Meiser - Montgomery [M] - Bois - Albert [M] - Midi(B) [M]

91 LOUISE [M] - Vanderkindere - Danco - [P] STALLE

92 ESPLANADE - Verboekhoven - Botanique [M] - Parc [M] - Louise [M] - Vanderkindere - FORT JACO

93 SCHAERBEEK(B) - Verboekhoven - Botanique [M] - Parc [M] - Louise [M] - Legrand - MARIE-JOSE

94 CIMETIERE JETTE - Bockstael(B) [M] - Liedts - Botanique [M] - Parc [M] - Louise [M] - Marie-José - WIENER

95 BOURSE [M] - Sablon - Pl. Royale - Trône [M] - Q. Léopold(B) - Cim. d'Ixelles - Keym - Wiener - HEILIGENBORRE

96 BOURSE [M] - Sablon - Pl. Royale - Trône [M] - Q.Léopold(B) - Cim. d'Ixelles - Keym - Archiducs - H.-Debroux [M] - STE-ANNE

98 HEROS - Stalle - [H] ERASME

MAIN STATIONS

BRUSSELS - SOUTH, rue de France - F8
BRUSSELS - CENTRAL, carrefour de l'Europe - I-J6
BRUSSELS - NORTH, rue du Progrès - J3
BRUSSELS - QUARTIER LEOPOLD, place du Luxembourg - K8
BRUSSELS - SCHAERBEEK, place Princesse Elisabeth
BRUSSELS - SCHUMANN, Rue de la Loi - M7

Travellers information : bureau : **203.28.80**

FOREIGN RAILWAYS

British Railways : rue de la Montagne 50 .... Tel. 548.00.40
Deutsche Bahn : rue du Luxembourg 23 .... Tel. 512.53.39
Chemins de Fer Italiens de l'Etat : pl. de Brouckère 46 .... Tel. 219.09.42

AIRLINE COMPANIES

National Airport : Zaventem.
Reservation, informations, confirmations .... Tel. 723.23.23
BATC-Airport Service : Brussels National Airport .... Tel. 753.39.13
Air Lingus (Irish Airl.) : rue du Trône 98 .... Tel. 548.98.48
Aéroflot : rue des Colonies 52b/54 .... Tel. 513.60.66
Air Canada (T.C.A.) : boulevard M. Lemonnier 131 .... Tel. 513.91.50
Air France : boulevard A. Max 48-50 .... Tel. 220.08.00
Air India : rue Ravenstein 50 .... Tel. 512.75.15
Alitalia : rue Cap. Crespel .... Tel. 513.88.93
British Airways : Aéroport Zaventem .... Tel. 720.71.43
C.S.A Czechoslovak Airlines : rue du Finistère 4 .... Tel. 217.17.92
Delta Air Lines : rue Colonel Bourg 128 .... Tel. 730.82.00
EL AL : rue de la Loi 28 .... Tel. 231.01.03
Iberia : place Stéphanie 10 .... Tel. 548.94.91
Icelandair : B.P. 56, 1060 Bruxelles .... Tel. 346.30.60
K.L.M.: B.P. 27, 1930 Zaventem .... Tel. 723.23.45
L.O.T. : rue de Namur 73a .... Tel. 502.53.00
Lufthansa : boulevard Anspach .... Tel. 212.09.22
Olympic Airways : avenue Louise 138a .... Tel. 649.81.58
Sabena : Aéroport de Bruxelles - National .... Tel. 723.23.23
S.A.S. : boulevard de la Woluwe 56 .... Tel. 720.59.76
South African Airways : rue du Finistère 4 .... Tel. 218.00.80
Swissair : place Madou 1 .... Tel. 220.71.11
Tunis-Air : Coudenberg 70 .... Tel. 512.23.15
Turkish Airlines : Cantersteen 51 .... Tel. 512.67.82
United Airlines : avenue Louise 350 .... Tel. 646.55.88
Virgin Express : Building 116 - Melsbroek Airport .... Tel. 752.05.05

STEAMSHIP LINES

Société nationale maritime Corse -Méditerranée - Ferryterranée
rue de la Montagne 52, 1000 Bruxelles .... Tel. 549.08.88

TOURIST INFORMATION

ADDRESSES

Telephone

Tourist Information of Brussels (T.I.B.) : Grand Place 1, 1000 B. 513.89.40
Tourism Centre :
rue du Marché-aux-Herbes 63, 1000 Bruxelles 504.03.90
Tourist Information Brabant (Flemish part) :
Diestsesteenweg 52,3010 Leuven 016/26.76.22
Royal Automobile Club Belgium (R.A.C.B.) :
rue d'Arlon 53, 1040 Br. 287.09.00
Touring Club Belgium (T.C.B.) : rue de la Loi 44, 1040 Br.. .... 233.22.11
Tourist Information Brabant (Walloon part) : chem. de Brux. 218, 1410 Waterloo
351.12.00

HOTELS

In Brussels you will find over 100 hotels (1 to 5 stars).
Reservations : B.T.R. (Belgique Tourisme Reservations)
Boulevard Anspach 111 - bte 4 - 1000 Bruxelles
Tél. 02/513.74.84 - Fax 02/513.92.77

YOUTH HOSTELS

JACQUES BREL :
rue de la Sablonnière 30, 1000 Bruxelles Tel. 281.01.87
BRUEGEL I.Y.H.F. : rue du Saint-Esprit 2, 1000 Bruxelles - Tel. 511.04.36
CENTRALE WALLONNE DES AUBERGES DE JEUNESSE :
rue Van Oost 52, 1030 Bruxelles - Tel. 215.31.00
C.H.A.B. : rue Traversière 8, 1210 Bruxelles - Tel. 217.01.58
ESPACE INTERNATIONALE :
chaussée de Wavre 205, 1050 Bruxelles - Tel.644.16.81
LA FONDERIE : rue de l'Eléphant 4, 1080 Bruxelles - Tel. 410.38.58
NEW SLEEP WELL : rue du Damier, 1000 Bruxelles - Tel. 218.50.50

RESTAURANTS

Because of its cosmopolitan character, Brussels offers a great number of exotic and traditional restaurants.

TOURISTIC AND BELGIAN SPECIALITIES
Petite rue des Bouchers, Grand Place and rue Haute.

FISH
place St.-Caherine.

ITALIAN
Quartier Schuman.

● *ARCHITECTURE ART NOUVEAU* ●

Horta Museum, rue Américaine 25, 1060 Bruxelles, Tél. 537.16.92
Belgian Comic Strip Centre, rue des Sables 20, 1000 Bruxelles, Tel. 219.19.80
Former Department Store Old England, rue Montagne de la Cour 2, 1000 Bruxelles

● *MARKETS* ●

Antiques : place du Grand Sablon (saturday and sunday)
Flea Market : place du Jeu de Balle (daily)
Alimentation : Gare du Midi (sunday)
place du Châtelain (wednesday)
Flowers and birds : Grand Place (sunday)

● *SHOPPING* ●

VARIOUS
rue Neuve, City 2, Gal. Agora, Gal. Centre Monnaie, rue Haute, av. de la Toison d'Or, Gal. Toison d'Or, Gal. Louise

LUXURY
avenue Louise, boulevard de Waterloo
Antiques : place du Grand Sablon

BELGIAN FASHION
rue Ant. Dansaert

BELGIAN SPECIALITIES
Belgian chocolates, Special beers, lace (Grand Place)

● *YEARLY EVENTS* ●

MAY - Royal Glasshouses of Laken
APRIL/MAY - Jazz Rally
MAY/JUNE - Queen Elisabeth International Music Competition
JULY - Ommegang (Historic procession)
- Brosella Folk and Jazz
- Munt Music
JULY/AUGUST - Cine Drive In
AUGUST - Memorial Van Damme
DECEMBER - Christmas in the city

VARIOUS INFORMATION

EUROPEAN ORGANIZATIONS

Commission of the European Communities :
rue Archimède 73 - 1040 Bruxelles - Tel. 295.38.44.
Economic and Social Committee :rue Ravenstein 2 - 1000 Bruxelles - Tel. 519.90.11.
Council European Communtiy : rue de la Loi 170 - 1040 Bruxelles - Tel. 234.61.11.
European parliament : rue Wiertz 43 - 1047 Bruxelles - Tel. 284.21.11.
Eurocontrol : rue de la Fusée 96 - 1130 Brux.- Tel. 729.90.11.
N.A.T.O. : Autoroute Bruxelles - Zaventem, 1110 Bruxelles. - Tel. 241.00.40.

PERMANENT REPRESENTATIONS

Austria : av. de Cortenberg 118	Tel. 441.21.11
Belgium : rue Belliard 62	Tel. 233.21.11
Denmark : rue d'Arlon 73	Tel. 233.08.11
Finland : rue de Trèves 100	Tel. 287.84.11
France : pl. de Louvain 14	Tel. 229.82.11
Germany : r. J. de Lalaing 19-21.	Tel. 238.18.11
Greece: av. de Cortenberg 71	Tel. 739.56.11
Ireland : av. Galilée 5	Tel. 218.06.05
Italy : rue du Marteau 5-11.	Tel. 220.04.11
Luxemburg : rue du Noyer 211	Tel. 735.20.60
Netherlands :av. Hermann-Debroux 48	Tel. 679.15.11
Portugal :rue Marie-Thèrese 11-13	Tel. 211.12.11
Spain : bld. du Régent 52	Tel. 509.86.11
Sweden : sq. de Meeûs 30	Tel. 289.56.11
United Kingdom : Rond point Schuman 6	Tel. 287.82.11

POST OFFICES

	Telephone
Anderlecht , 1070 - rue de Veeweyde 15	521.62.40
Auderghem, 1160 - chaussée de Wavre 1212	672.79.09
Berchem-Sainte-Agathe, 1082 - avenue Josse Goffin 12	465.80.41
Brussels, 1000 - Centre Monnaie	226.21.11
Brussels, 1020 - rue Tielemans 32	426.32.45
Brussels, 1040 - avenue de Cortenberg 16	282.99.12
Brussels, 1110 - O.T.A.N.	726.89.90
Brussels, 1120 - pl. Peter Benoit 13	268.23.08
Brussels, 1130 - rue de Verdun 224	216.29.33
Etterbeek, 1040 - chaussée St-Pierre 124	648.04.42
Evere, 1140 - avenue du Cimetière de Brux. 35	726.60.47
Forest, 1190 - rue P. Decoster 88	344.92.11

Ganshoren, 1083 - rue A. et M. Hellinckx 26 .... 426.30.10
Ixelles, 1050 - chaussée d'Ixelles 27 .... 511.98.90
Jette, 1090 - rue E. De Smet 8 .... 479.37.99
Koekelberg, 1081 - rue de l'Armistice 9 .... 426.23.40
Molenbeek, 1080 - chaussée de Ninove 122 .... 410.62.41
Saint-Gilles 1060 - chaussée de Charleroi 33 .... 539.19.62
Saint-Josse-Ten-Noode, 1210 - rue Willems 18 .... 230.57.39
Schaerbeek, 1030 - rue Royale Ste-Marie 98 .... 216.29.74
Uccle, 1180 - chaussée d'Alsemberg 1069 .... 332.09.46
Watermael-Boitsfort, 1170 - rue Ph.Dewolfs 8 .... 672.03.22
Woluwe-Saint-Lambert, 1200 - av. G. Henri 328 .... 733.37.33
Woluwe-Saint-Pierre, 1150 - dr. de Nivelles 128 .... 672.79.29

To send a telegram by telephone, call : **1325**

Anti Poison Centre : (070) 245 245

GENDARMERIE

Urgent call 101

General Staff, General Services, rue F. Toussaint 47 B5 .... 642.61.11
Region Brabant Legion Mobile 642.61.11
Territorial group Brabant, ... 507.92.11
District BOB Brigade Brussels, rue de la Croix de Fer 77, 1000 Br. 507.92.11
Brigades :
Anderlecht, r. V. Rauter 259 A 521.15.25
Auderghem-Watermael-Boitsfort, av. du Kouter 87 .... 672.29.13
Berchem-Ganshoren-Jette-Koekelberg-Molenbeek,
av. Charles-Quint 293 .... 468.22.24
Brussels-City-Etterbeek-Ixelles-St-Gilles, rue de la Croix de Fer 77 .... 507.92.11
Brussels II, r. Stéphanie 87 .... 426.11.15
Evere-Schaerbeek-St-Josse, rue Jan Blockx 22-24 .... 215.32.33
Forest-Uccle, av. Fort-Jaco 22 .... 374.35.29
Woluwe-St-Lambert/St-Pierre, rue D. Van Bever 6 .... 762.93.37

POLICE

Police -emergency **101**

Ambulance
Accidents **100**
Fire-brigade

	Telephone
Anderlecht : Central Div. : r. Démosthène 36	521.01.70
Auderghem : rue E. Idiers 12	676.49.14
Berchem-Sainte-Agathe : rue Hubert Blauwet 26	464.04.15
Brussels : *All services* : rue du Marché au Charbon 30	517.96.11
Etterbeek : Chaussée St.-Pierre 122	627.22.22
Evere : Sq. S. Hoedemaekers 10	247.64.00
Forest : rue de Liège 1	370.23.11
Ganshoren : av. Van Overbeke 163	427.43.47
Ixelles : Central Div. (Town Hall)	513.65.00
Jette : Place Cardinal Mercier 11	423.14.00
Koekelberg : rue George-dit-Marchal 2	414.10.85
Molenbeek-St-Jean : rue du Facteur 2	412.38.00
Saint-Gilles : rue A. Breart 104	536.13.11
Saint-Josse-Ten-Noode : 1e div., rue de Bériot 2a	220.27.00
Schaerbeek : Central Div., pl. Colignon	243.87.11
Uccle : Central Div., rue A. Danse 3	348.66.11
Watermael-Boitsfort : drève du Duc 2	674.74.74
Woluwe-Saint-Lambert : rue F. Debelder 15-17	761.29.54
Woluwe-Saint-Pierre : avenue Ch. Thielemans 93	773.05.00

RELIGIONS

ANGLICAN

The United Anglican Church (Church of England), rue Capitaine Crespel 29, 1050 Brussels.

ROMAN CATHOLIC

Cathedral Sts-Michel and Gudule, Parvis Ste-Gudule.
Notre-Dame des Victoires - Sablon.
Notre-Dame de la Chapelle, place de la Chapelle
Saint-Nicolas, rue au Beurre
Saint-Jean-Baptiste au Béguinage, Finistère, rue Neuve

PROTESTANTS

Eglise du Musée, rue du Musée 2, 1000 Brussels
Dutch Evangelical Church, place du Nouveau Marché aux Grains 8
St-Andrews Church (Church of Scotland), chaussée de Vleurgat 181, 1050 Brussels
American Protestant Church of Brussels (Eglise Méthodiste), Kattenberg 19, 1170 Brussels

JEWISH

Synagogue, rue de la Régence 32, 1000 Brussels
Synagogue, rue Dethy 73, 1060 Brussels.

ORTHODOX
Russian, avenue De Fré 19, 1180 Bruxelles.
Greek, avenue de Stalingrad, 1000 Bruxelles.

CHRISTIAN SCIENCE
Chaussée de Vleurgat 96, 1050 Bruxelles.

ISLAMIC
Centre Islamique, Parc du Cinquantenaire 14, 1040 Bruxelles

• *EMBASSIES* •

Algeria : av. Molière 209, 1060 Brussels .... Tél. 343.50.78.
Angola : rue Franz Merjay 182, 1050 Brussels .... Tél. 346.18.80.
Argentina : av. Louise 225, 1050 Brussels .... Tél. 647.78.12.
Australia : rue Guimard 6, 1040 Brussels .... Tél. 231.05.00.
Austria : rue de l'Abbaye 47, 1050 Brussels .... Tél. 649.91.70.
Bangladesh : rue Jordaens 29, 1000 Brussels .... Tel. 640.55.00.
Bolivia : av. Louise 176, 1050 Brussels .... Tel. 647.27.18.
Brazil : av. Louise 350, 1050 Brussels .... Tel. 640.20.15.
Bulgaria : av. Hamoir 58, 1180 Brussels .... Tel. 374.59.63.
Burundi : square Marie-Louise 46, 1000 Brussels .... Tel. 230.45.35.
Canada : av. de Tervueren 2, 1040 Brussels .... Tel. 741.06.11.
Chile : rue Montoyer 40, 1000 Brussels .... Tel. 280.16.20.
China : av. de Tervueren 443, 1150 Brussels .... Tel. 771.26.81.
Cuba : avenue Roberts Jones 77, 1180 Brussels .... Tel. 343.00.20.
Cyprus : sq. Ambiorix 2, 1000 Brussels .... Tel. 735.35.10.
Czech Republic : rue Engeland 555, 1180 Brussels .... Tel. 374.12.03.
Denmark : avenue Louise 221, 1050 Brussels .... Tel. 648.25.25.
Egypt : avenue L. Errera 44, 1180 Brussels .... Tel. 345.50.15.
El Salvador : avenue de Tervueren 171, 1150 Brussels .... Tel. 733.04.85.
Finland : rue de Trèves 100, 1040 Brussels .... Tel. 287.84.11.
France : rue Ducale 65, 1000 Brussels .... Tel. 548.87.11.
Germany : av. de Tervueren 190, 1150 Brussels .... Tel. 774.19.11.
Great-Britain : rue d'Arlon 85, 1040 Brussels .... Tel. 287.62.11.
Greece : avenue Louise 430, 1050 Brussels .... Tel. 646.55.51.
Hungary : rue E. Picard 41, 1050 Brussels .... Tel. 343.67.90.
India : chaussée de Vleurgat 217, 1050 Brussels .... Tel. 640.91.40.
Indonésia : avenue de Tervueren 294, 1150 Br. .... Tel. 771.20.14.
Irak : avenue des Aubépines 23, 1180 Brussels .... Tel. 374.59.92.
Iran : avenue de Tervueren 415, 1150 Brussels .... Tel. 762.37.45.
Ireland: rue de Froissart 89, 1040 Brussels .... Tel. 230.53.37.
Iceland : rue de Trèves 74, 1040 Brussels .... Tel. 286.17.00.
Israel : avenue de l'Observatoire 40, 1180 Brussels .... Tél. 373.55.11.
Italy : rue E. Claus 28, 1050 Brussels .... Tel. 649.97.00.
Japan : avenue des Arts 58, 1000 Brussels .... Tel. 513.23.40.

Kenya : avenue de la Joyeuse Entrée 1, 1040 Brussels .... Tel. 230.30.65.
Korea : av. Hamoir 3, 1180 Brussels .... Tel. 375.39.80.
Liban : rue G. Stocq 2, 1050 Brussels .... Tel. 649.94.60.
Luxemburg : rue du Noyer 211, 1000 Brussels .... Tel. 733.99.77.
Malta : rue Lejeune 44, 1060 Brussels .... Tel. 343.01.95.
Mexico : avenue F. Roosevelt 99, 1050 Brussels .... Tel. 629.07.11.
Monaco : place G. d'Arezzo 17, 1180 Brussels .... Tel. 347.49.87.
Morocco : boulevard Saint-Michel 29, 1040 Brussels .... Tel. 732.65.45.
Norway : avenue Louise 130a, 1050 Brussels .... Tel. 646.07.80.
Netherlands: avenue Hermann-Debroux 48, 1160 Brussels .... Tel. 679.17.11.
Poland : avenue des Gaulois 29, 1040 Brussels .... Tel. 735.72.12.
Portugal : avenue de la Toison d'Or 55, 1060 Brussels .... Tel. 539.37.13.
Rumania : rue Gabrielle 105, 1180 Brussels .... Tel. 345.00.40.
Russia : avenue De Fré 66, 1180 Brussels .... Tel. 374.34.00.
Saudi Arabia : av. Fr. Roosevelt 45, 1050 Brussels .... Tel. 649.57.25.
Slovakia : avenue Brugmann 118, 1190 Brussels .... Tel. 343.35.05.
South-Africa : rue de la Loi 26/b7 1040 Brussels .... Tel. 285.44.00.
Spain : rue de la Science 19, 1040 Brussels .... Tel. 230.03.40.
Sweden: avenue Louise 148, 1050 Brussels .... Tel. 289.57.60.
Switzerland : rue de la Loi 26, 1040 Brussels .... Tel. 285.43.50.
Syria : avenue Fr. Roosevelt 3, 1050 Brussels .... Tel. 648.01.39.
Tunisia : avenue de Tervueren 278, 1150 Brussels .... Tel. 771.73.95.
Turkey : rue Montoyer 4, 1000 Brussels .... Tel. 513.40.95.
United States of America : boulevard du Régent 27,
1000 Brussels .... Tel. 513.38.30.
Zaire: rue Marie de Bourgogne 30, 1000 Brussels .... Tel. 513.66.10.

● *CONSULATES* ●

Algeria : rue de Lausanne 30-32, 1060 Brussels .... Tel. 537.81.33.
Czech Republic : avenue A. Buyl 154, 1050 Brussels .... Tel. 647.58.98.
Finland : avenue des Gaulois 7, 1040 Brussels .... Tel. 743.13.60.
France : place de Louvain 12a, 1000 Brussels .... Tel. 229.85.00.
Great-Britain : rue d'Arlon 85, 1040 Brussels .... Tel. 287.62.11
Iceland : Galerie Ravenstein 27, 1000 Brussels .... Tel. 512.59.65.
Italy : rue de Livourne 38, 1000 Brussels .... Tel. 537.19.34.
Liberia : place De Brouckère 31, 1000 Brussels .... Tel. 217.23.00.
Morocco : avenue Van Volxem 18, 1190 Brussels .... Tel. 346.19.66.
Peru : rue des Pierres 29, 1000 Brussels .... Tel. 511.60.63.
Poland : rue des Francs 28, 1040 Brussels .... Tel. 736.04.64.
Turkey : rue Montoyer 4, 1000 Brussels .... Tel. 513.40.95.
Tunisia : Boulevard St. Michel 103, 1040 Brussels .... Tel. 731.61.02.
Uruguay : avenue des Vaillants 17, 1200 Brussels .... Tel. 731.61.02.

PARKINGS

*** (Covered)**

* Albertine : place de la Justice 16.
* Botanique : boulevard du Jardin Botanique 29-31.
* City 2 : bld. du Jardin Botanique 29
* Ecuyer : rue de l'Ecuyer 11-17.
* Evêque 58 : rue de l'Evêque 1.
Galerie Louise : rue Cap.Crespel 27.
Louise Concorde : rue d.l. Concorde 66.
* Manhattan : rue des Croisades 19.
* Monnaie : place de la Monnaie.
* Parking des 2 Portes : Bd. de Waterloo 2a.
Parking Philips : pl. de Brouckère 2.
* Passage 44 : rue de l'Ommegang 16.
* Rogier : pl. Rogier
Saint-Jean : bd. du Jardin Botanique.

SPORTS

PARKS AND GARDENS

	PLAN
Bois de la Cambre	H.P.
Parc Royal ou Parc de Bruxelles	J 6
Parc du Palais d'Egmont	I 8
Parc du Cinquantenaire	NO 7
Parc Josaphat	N 3
Jardin Botanique	K 4
Jardin du Petit Sablon	I 8
Jardin du Mont des Arts	I 7

STADIUMS

Brussels : Stade Roi Baudouin, avenue du Marathon 135.

FOOTBALL

Belgian Football Federation, Maison du Football, av. H de Strooper 145, Tél. 477.12.11

RUGBY

Belgian Rugby Federation : avenue Rogier, Tél. 216.40.24

HOCKEY

International Hockey Federation : av. des Arts 1, Tél. 219.45.37

TENNIS

Royal Belgian Lawn Tennis Federation : Pass. Internationale 6 Bte. 522, Tél.217.22.00

POOLS

Calypso : avenue Léopold Wiener 60
Oceade : Bruparck
Poseidon : avenue des Vaillants 2
Bains de Bruxelles : rue du Chevreuil 28
Bains de Ganshoren : place Fabiola 10
Bains d'Ixelles : rue de la Natation
Bains L. Nameche : (Molenbeek) rue Van Kalck 93
Bains de Saint-Gilles : Rue de la Perche 38
Bains de Schaerbeek : r. de Jérusalem 54
Sport Centre Etterbeek : rue des Champs 69

SKATING

Ice Skating (Forest National) : avenue du Globe 36
Ice Skating Poséidon : : avenue des Vaillants 2, 1200 Bruxelles

BOWLING

Crosly Super Bowling : quai au Foin 43, Tél. 217.28.01
Crosly Super Bowling : boulevard de l'Empereur 36, Tél. 512.08.74

CAMPINGSITES

Beersel : Ukkelsteenweg 75
Grimbergen : Veldkantstraat 64
Huizingen : Domaine Provincial
Paul Rosmant : Warandeberg, Wezembeek-Oppem

GOLF COURSES

Anderlecht Golf Club : rue Scholle 1, 1070 Brussels, Tél. 521.16.87
Brussels Golf Club : chaussée de la Hulpe 53a, 1170 Brussels, Tél. 672.22.22
Golf Club de Sept Fontaines : chaussée d'Alsemberg 1021, 14210 Braine l'Alleud, Tél. 353.02.46
Golf Practice Rhode St.-Genèse : avenue Brassine 92, 1640 Rhode-Saint-Genèse, Tél. 358.34.67

STAGES AND ENTERTAINMENTS

ATELIER SAINTE-ANNE : rue des Tanneurs 75-77, 1000 Brussels .... T.548.02.66.
AUDITORIUM 44 : bouleard du Jardin Botanique 44, 1000 Brussels .. T.218.27.35.
BEURSSCHOUWBURG : rue A. Orts 22, 1000 Brussels .... T.513.82.90.
CIRQUE ROYAL : rue de l'Enseignement 81,1000 Brussels .... T.218.20.15.
COMEDIE C. VOLTER : av. Frères Legrain 98, 1150 SPW .... T.762.09.63.
COMPAGNIE YVAN BAUDOUIN (THEATRE) :
avenue d'Auderghem 221, 1040 Ett .... T.640.27.60.
CONSERVATOIRE ROYAL DE MUSIQUE :
rue de la Régence 30, 1000 Brussels .... T.511.04.27.
FOREST NATIONAL : avenue du Globe 36, 1190 Forest .... T.345.03.55.
HALLES DE SCHAERBEEK : rue Royale Ste-Marie 22a, 1030 Sch .... T.218.00.31.
JEUNE THEATRE DE L'ULB :
Cité de l'ULB, av. Paul Heger 22, 1000 Brussels .... T.640.69.27.
KAAITHEATER : Quai des Péniches 2, 1000 Brussels .... T.201.58.58.
KONINKLIJK CONSERVATORIUM BRUSSEL:
rue de la Régence 30, 1000 Brussels .... T.513.45.87.
KONINKLIJKE VLAAMSE SCHOUWBURG (K.V.S.) :
rue de Laeken 146 - 1000 Brussels .... T.217.69.37.

MAISON DU SPECTACLE DE LA BELLONE :
rue de Flandre 46, 1000 Brussels T.513 33 33
MEDIATHEQUE DE LA COMMUNAUTE FRANCAISE DE BELGIQUE : Passage
44, bld. du Jardin Botanique 44, 1000 Brussels .... T.218.25.99.
MOLIERE (THEATRE) : gal.de la Porte de Namur 22, 1050 Ixelles ..... T.513.58.00.
MUNTSCHOUWBURG (OPERA) :
place de la Monnaie, 1000 Brussels .... T.229.12.11.
NOUVEAU THEATRE DE BELGIQUE :
rue du Viaduc 122, 1050 Ixelles .... T.640.84.37.
NOUVEAU THEATRE DE QUAT'SOUS :
rue de la Violette 28b, 1000 Brussels .... T.512.10.22.
OPERA NATIONAL - T.R.M. : place de la Monnaie, 1000 Brussels ..... T.229.12.11.
PALAIS DES BEAUX ARTS : rue Ravenstein 23, 1000 Brussels .... T.507.82.00.
PARC (THEATRE ROYAL DU PARC) :
rue de la Loi 3, 1000 Brussels .... T.512.53.43.
RIDEAU DE BRUXELLES (THEATRE DU) :
rue Ravenstein 23, 1000 Brussels .... T.507.83.60.
THEATRE 140 : avenue E. Plasky 140, 1030 Sc .... T.733.97.08.
THEATRE DE LA BALSAMINE : avenue F. Marchal 1, 1030 Sc .... T.733.04.64.
THEATRE DE LA VIE : rue Traversière 45, 1210 Brussels .... T.218.79.35.
THEATRE DE POCHE : chem. du Gymnase 1a - 1050 Brussels .... T.649.17.27.
THEATRE DU MERIDIEN : rue d'Aumale 2, 1070 An .... T.522.73.30.
THEATRE DU PLAN K : galerie de la Reine 2, 1000 Brussels .... T.511.83.01.
THEATRE DU RESIDENCE-PALACE : rue de la Loi 155, 1040 B ..... T.231.03.05.
THEATRE IMPOPULAIRE : rue Leys 42, 1040 Brl .... T.733.00.93.
THEATRE NATIONAL DE LA COM. FRANÇAISE DE BELGIQUE :
place Rogier, 1210 Brussels .... T.203.28.95.
THEATRE POEME : rue d'Ecosse 30, 1060 SGi .... T.538.63.57.
THEATRE ROYAL DES GALERIES : Galerie du Roi 32, 1000 B ...... T.513.39.60.
THEATRE VARIA : rue du Sceptre 78, 1040 Brussels .... T.640.35.50.
THEATRE XL : rue Goffart 7a - 1050 Ixelles .... T.230.48.78.
THEATRON : rue Leys 46, 1000 Brussels .... T.733.68.69.
TOONE (THEATRE DE) : Petite rue des Bouchers 21, 1000 Brussels .. T.511.71.37.

● *CULTURAL CENTRES* ●

MUNICIPAL CENTRE JOLI BOIS av. du Haras 100, 1150 SPW .... T.771.91.22.
CULTURAL CENTRE - CENTENAIRE : Cité Modèle Bloc 3 .... T.479.84.99.
CULTURAL CENTRE AUDERGHEM :
bd du Souverain 185, 1160 Aud .... T.660.03.03.
CULTURAL AND ARTISTIC CENTRE UCCLE :
rue Rouge 47, 1180 Uck .... T.374.64.84.
CULTURAL CENTRE JACQUES FRANCK :
ch. de Waterloo 94, 1060 SGi .... T.538.90.20.
INTELLECTUAL CENTRE ANDERLECHT :
rue du Chapelain 3, 1070 And T.521 62 08

FRENCH COMMUNITY "LE BOTANIQUE" :
rue Royale 236, 1210 SJN .... T.226.12.11.
CULTURAL ANDERLECHT : rue d'Aumole 67, 1070 And .... T. 522.74.07.
FONDATION JACQUES BREL : Vieille Halle aux Blés 11, 1000 Brl T. 203.36.75.
WOLUWE-SAINT-PIERRE : av. Ch. Tielemans 93, 1150 SPW .... T. 521.62.08.

● *CINEMAS* ●

BRUSSELS CENTRE

ACTOR'S STUDIO (2 salles) : petite rue des Bouchers 16 .... T.512.16.96.
ARENBERG (2 salles) : gal. de la Reine 26 .... T.512.80.63.
AVENTURE (3 salles) : gal. du Centre 57 .... T.219.17.48.
MUSEE DU CINEMA : rue Baron Horta 9 .... T.507.83.70.
U.G.C. - DE BROUCKERE (10 salles) :
pl. de Brouckère 38, 1000 Br .... T.(0900) 29 .930.

BRUSSELS TOWN

ACROPOLE - U.G.C. : galerie de la Toison d'Or 17 .... T.(0900) 29.930.
VENDOME/LE ROYE (4 salles) : Ch. de Wavre 18 .... T.512.65.53.

BRUSSELS HEYSEL

KINEPOLIS (26 salles) :Bruparck-Heysel .... T.474.26.00.

BRUPARC

This recreation area is situated a 100 meters away from the Atomium near the "Parc des Expositions". **Tel. 02/ 477.03.77 - Fax. 02/478.03.96**

* Mini-Europe : picture of the members of the European community - with historical and contemporary buildings, traffic on the roads and trains, ports, canals, airports etc....
The entity is situated in beautiful green surroundings.

* Oceade - Tel. 02/478.43.20
The biggest covered waterfun centre of Belgium offers the visitors the necessary leisure in an exotic, adventureful entourage.
Waterfun : wavebath, big dipper, cannon, balls, massagerays, bubblebaths, open-air-baths, water cannon, etc....

* Kinepolis - Tél 02/478.04.50
Unique in Belgium : a centre of 26 halls with one specially reserved to project pageant films on a screen of 600 m2.

* The village
The village forms the heart of Bruparck and is erected in "Old Brussels"-style.
Here is, througout the year, from morning till dawn, "something going on".

RUE DES CHAPELIERS

RUE CHARLES BULS
To the Manneken-Pis Fountain

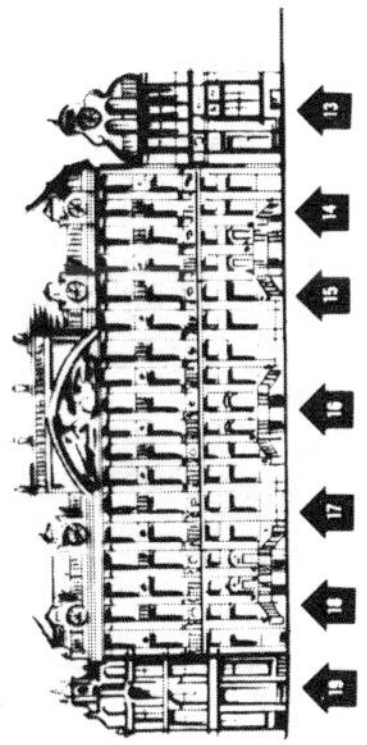

1-2. **THE KING OF SPAIN (LE ROI D'ESPAGNE) 1696-1697**
3. **THE WHEEL BARROW (LA BROUETTE) 1696**
4. **THE SACK (LE SAC) 1697**
5. **THE SHE-WOLF (LA LOUVE) 1696**
6. **THE HORN (LE CORNET) 1697**
7. **THE FOX (LE RENARD) 1699**
TOWN HALL (HOTEL DE VILLE)
8. **THE STAR (L'ETOILE) 1852**
9. **THE SWAN (LE CYGNE) 1698**
10. **THE GOLDEN TREE (L'ARBRE D'OR) 1696**
11. **THE ROSE (LA ROSE) 1702**
12. **THE MOUNT TABOR (LE MONT TABOR) 1699**
13. **THE RENOWNED HOUSE OF THE DUKES OF BRABANT 1698**
14. **THE HERMITAGE (L'ERMITAGE)**
15. **THE FORTUNE (LA FORTUNE)**
16. **THE WINDMILL (LE MOULIN A VENT)**

RUE DE LA COLLINE
To the Saint-Michael's Cathedral
and Central Station

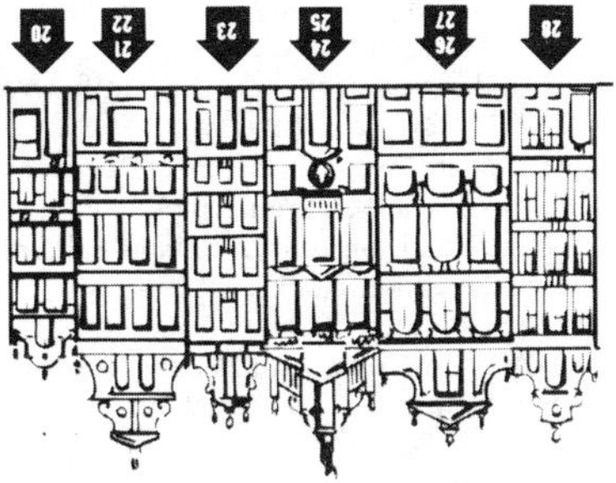

RUE DES HARENGS

RUE DE LA TETE D'OR
To the South station

17. THE PEWTER-POT (LE POT D'ETAIN)
18. THE HILL (LA COLLINE)
19. THE PURSE (LA BOURSE)
THE SCALES (LA BALANCE) 1704
20. THE KITE (LE CERF VOLANT) 1696
21-22. JOSEPH AND ANNE (JOSEPH ET ANNE) 1696
23. THE ANGEL (L'ANGE) 1696
24-25. THE GOLDEN GALLEON OR THE MOLE (LA CHALOUPE D'OR OU LA TAUPE) 1698
26-27. THE PIGEON (LE PIGEON) 1697
28. SMALL ROOM OF THE AMMAN (LA CHAMBRETTE DE L'AMMAN) 1696
THE KING HOUSE (MAISON DU ROI) 1873
34. THE HELM (LE HEAUME)
35. THE PEACOCK (LE PAON)
36. THE LITTLE FOX (LE PETIT RENARD)
37. THE OAK (LE CHENE)
38. THE SAINTE BARBE (SAINTE BARBE)
39. THE ASS (L'ANE)

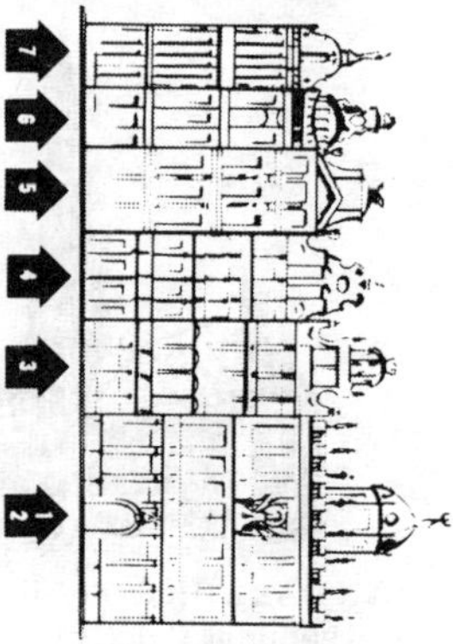

RUE AU BEURRE
To the Stock Exchange

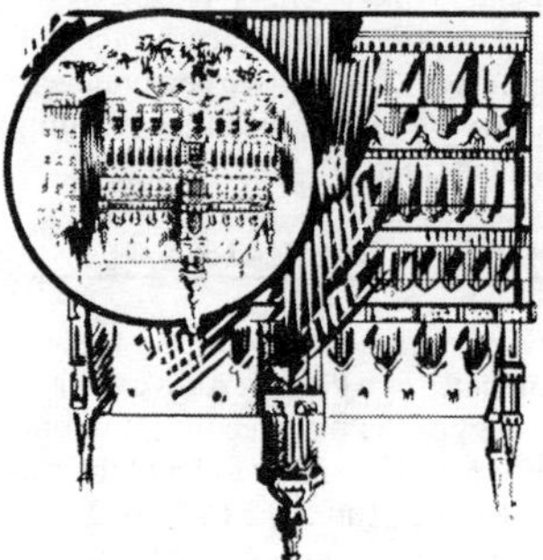

RUE CHAIR ET PAIN

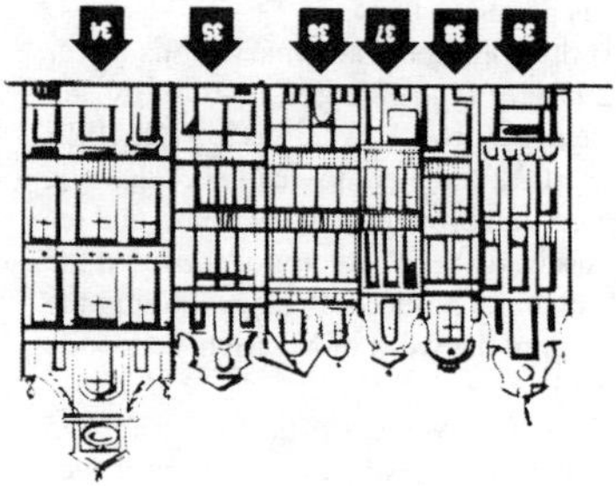

Situated on former marshland, it was a centre of social, economics, and politics of the town from the XIIth century.
More or less entirely destroyed in 48 hours on the 13th and 14th of August 1695 by the artillery of Marshal de VILLEROY by order of Louis XIV (the Sun King).
In less than four years however (1696-1700) the powerful trade corporations had courageously rebuilt their splendid houses in a blend of Italian and Flemish "Baroque Style".
The Grand Place, already a beautiful sight during the daytime, takes of Fairy-Art after sunset with the illuminations magnifying the beauty of the architecture.
SEASON FROM JUNE TO SEPTEMBER FROM 9 PM. SPECTACLE OF MUSIC AND ILLUMINATIONS.

TOWN HALL (Hôtel de Ville) - Ogival gothique style(I 6).

The left wing, the oldest part, dates from 1402, is the work of Jacob van Tienen : the right wing, by an unknwon architect, was begun in 1444.
At the sommet of the marvellous tower (295 feet high) erected in 1449 by Jan Van Ruysbroeck, architect to PHILIPPE LE BON, is a gigantic weather cock made of golden bronze, (16 feet high), and representing the Protector of the town the Archangel Saint Michael grounding the Dragon, the work of Maarten Van Rode in 1454.
This edifice was partly destroyed in 1695 during the siege of the town by the armies of LOUIS XIV (Sun King) under the command of Marshal de Villeroy.

1.-2. THE KING OF SPAIN - 1696-1697

Baker's House.
Dome of italian inspiration surmounted by a FAME. The facade is adorned by a bust of CHARLES II the king of Spain, and by four medaillions representing the effigy of roman emperors. Above the front door a golden bust of Saint Hubert (Patron Saint of the bakers).

3. THE WHEEL BARROW - 1696

Greaser's House.
On the pediment, the statue of Saint Gilles (Patron saint of grease dealers).

4. THE SACK - 1697

Carpenters and coopers' House.
The facade is decorated by carpenters and coopers tools, also by two personnages : one carrying a sack, the other plunging both hands in it.

5. THE SHE WOLF - 1696

The archers house.
Surmounted by a Phenix. Above the door bas-relief of the wolf feeding Romulus and Remus. To remark as well, the statues of : The Truth, The Lie, The Peace and the Discord, surmounted by medal-

lions representing the emperors Trojan, Tibire, Auguste, Cesar.

6. THE HORN - 1697

Boatmen's house.
The gable has the shape of a ships poop (XVIIth century). Decorative theme, life of sailors represented by sea-horses, Tritons and Dolphins. Medallions with effigy of CHARLES II, king of Spain, and four figures symbolising the four winds.

7. THE FOX - 1699

Haberdashers' house.
Surmounted by the statue of Saint-Nicolas (Patron saint of the haberdashers) in golden copper. Bas-relief : children dealing with the occupation of this corporation. Statue of the Justice and of the four parts of the world .

8. THE STAR - 1852

Chief Justice house (Amman).
From this house, XIII century, the judge surveyed all capital executions. The Lord Everaert 't Serclaes, alderman of the town, died here, following an assault in 1388. Under the arches a bas-relief in bronze commemorates his martyr.

9. THE SWAN - 1698 (Louis XIV style)

Butchers' house.
Originally a cabaret surrounded by gardens.

10. THE GOLDEN TREE - 1696

Tanners' house, followed by unpholsterets became finally brewers' house.

A fine statue of CHARLES DE LORRAINE, Governor of Holland tops the house. The bas-relief represents the vintages and hop picking. This home contains a magnificent Brewery Museum.

11. THE ROSE - 1702

Private residence.
Retains its name from the family Van der Rosen who lived there in the XVth centruy.

12. THE MOUNT TABOR - 1699

The Three Colours.
This home was the properly of private citizens.

13. THE RENOWNED

The King of Bavaria (rue des Chapeliers).
The entrance is topped by a golden satue. In the centre the bust of Cambrinus, on his left "The Wheat" as well as the Hops on his right.

14 - 15 - 16 - 17 - 18 - 19. HOUSE OF THE DUKES OF BRABANT - 1698

The architecture recalls the style of italian palaces. In reality it groups six houses all similar, of which the nineteen pilasters support the bust of former kings (when the HOUSE OF DUKES) These houses are named : 14. The Hermitage (Saint Anthony Hermit) - 15. The Fortune (reunion place of the tanners) - 16. The Windmill (belonging to the millers) - 17. The Pewter-Pot (reunion place to the carpenters) - 18. The Hill, in this house was established the guild of the four crowned, that is : sculptors, Stone Cutters, Masons and Slaters. - 19. Purse.

THE SCALES - 1704

Situated : rue de la Colline. Two negroes support the balcony, and two small angels one of them holding the scales.

20. THE KITE - 1696

Its sign is on the gable, corner of the rue de la Colline.

21.-22. JOSEPH AND ANNE - 1696

Originally built in wood - 1594.

23. THE ANGEL - 1696

Formely belonged to the Abbey of Forest, beginning of XVIth century.

24. THE GOLDEN GALLEON or THE MOLE - 1698

Tailors' house.
On the gable, the statue of the Bishop Saint Boniface and over the entrance door a statue of Sainte Barbe.

26.-27 THE PIGEON - 1697

Painters' house.
Victor Hugo stayed here on the second floor in 1852 during his exile after the fall of the French Government on the 2nd December 1851.

28. SMALL ROOM OF THE AMMAN'S (Judge) - 1696

Today called "Aux Armes de Brabant" because of the coat of arms which adorns the facade.

THE KINGS HOUSE - 1873 - Style Flamboyant.

The Bread House in the XIIIth century.
Was successively DUKES HOUSE and KINGS HOUSE in the XVth century. It became known as the Peoples' House in 1794 under french domination. Destroyed in 1872 and rebuilt in 1873 by the architect Jamaer. One can remark the central arcade with its statues of : Marie de Bourgogne, Charles-Quint, Henry 1st, Jean 1st, as well as the armouries of Brabant (Lion) and Austria (Eagle).
Actually a Communal Museum. It contains very interesting collections consecrated to Brussels History and Archeology.

A group of Flemish Baroque Style Houses :

34. THE HELM

35. THE PEACOCK

36. THE LITTLE FOX

37. THE OAK

38. THE SAINTE BARBE

39. THE ASS

THE CHURCH OF NOTRE-DAME DU BON SECOURS (H6)

One of the most gracious Flemish Renaissance churches, it is nevertheless the one which is the furthest from the typical Flemish style in the hexagonal form of its plan and its short naves. The coasts of arms which decorate it are those of Charles of Lorraine.

THE EUROPEAN COMMUNITIES(M7)

It was in 1958 that the headquarters of the European Communities and Euratom were established in Brussels. Built between 1963 and 1969 by the architect de Vestel, the building, called the Berlaymont, takes the form of a four-pointed star.

THE EGMONT PALACE (I8)

Built in the 16th century, it was profoundly altered in the 18th century by the family of the Dukes of Arenberg. Some famous personalities stayed here : Queen Christine of Sweden, Louis XV, Jean-Baptiste Rousseau and Voltaire. Property of the Ministry of Foreign Affairs. Only the gardens are accessible.

THE CHURCH OF SAINT-JOHN THE BAPTIST IN THE BEGUINAGE(H4-5)

Attributed to the architect L. Fay-d'Herbe, this church is a remarkable illustration of the 17th century Italo-Flemish Baroque style. Its facade is considered one of the most beautiful in Belgium.

THE ANGLE TOWER(I7)

This remaining section of the 12th century ramparts stands next to the gate where the guild leader François Anneessens was imprisoned before his execution in 1719.

THE BLACK TOWER(H5)

This tower formed part of the first ramparts constructed in the 12th century, and is a typical example of the towers in this wall.

SAINT-CATHERINES TOWER (H5)

Of the old 17th century church only this tower remains.

THE CHURCH OF NOTRE DAME DU FINISTERE (I4)

This 18th century church is built on the site of a chapel founded in the 15th century and called "Venstersterre". A Gothic virgin, Notre-Dame du Bon Succès, is venerated here.

THE CHURCH OF THE MADELEINE (I6)

The Baroque façade of the former Chapel of Saint-Anne, was added to this charming 15 th century Gothic oratory.

THE SAINT-HUBERT ROYAL GALLERIES(I6)

These covered arcades, flanked by shops were built in 1846 from the plans of the architect J.P. Cluysenaer. The construction of these shopping galleries was a "European Première". They are made up of three distinct parts, The Galerie du Roi, The Galerie de la Reine and The Galerie des Princes.

THE PARC DES EXPOSITIONS

This is a unique complex in Europe for trade-fairs and expositions. It contains the headquarters of the Brussels International Fair as well as the halls formerly called "Palais du centenaire". Built in 1935, they commemorate the centenary of Belgian Independence. This complex hosted the universal exposition in 1935 and the world expo in 1958. A little further, towards the right, the vast building of the **"Brussels International Trade Mart"** dates from 1975. This is the marketplace for professionals.
Finally, one can visit **Bruparc** (bd. du Centenaire 20 - Brussels), the capital's new leisure Centre, with Mini-Europe, Oceadium (water-fun park), Kinepolis (the largest cinema complex in the world) and The Village (old Brussels style).

THE ROYAL PALACE OF LAEKEN

This palace in the Louis XVI style is the residence of our sovereigns. Built on the site of an old manor house, bought by the governors Marie-Christine and Albert of Saxen-Techen, Napoleon resided there and signed the Peace treaty with Russia. (Can not be visited).

NATIONAL ARCHIVES(I7)

"Through the country's history"
Two hundred selected items, with a systematic, in-depth commentary. The eldest document dates from 819.

THE CHURCH OF SAINT-CATHERINE (H5)

Built on the site of an old 17th century church, it was designed by the architects Poelaert and Janssens and aims at originality through a mixture of various styles. The collection of paintings makes this church worth visiting.

THE CHURCH OF SAINT-JACQUES ON COUDENBERG (J7)

Its façade is an exact replica of a Roman peristyle. During the French Revolution, it was converted into a temple of reason and then a temple of the law, before returning to Catholic worship in 1802.

THE CHURCH OF NOTRE-DAME-DES VICTOIRES DU-SABLON (I7)

This precious example of the flourishing of flamboyant Gothic art in Belgium owes its magnificence to the Crossbowmen of the City who built it in the 15th century. It was built on the spot of a 14th century chapel, to worship the miraculous statue made by Baet Soetkens in Antwerp and brought to Brussels in 1348.

THE CHURCH OF THE TRINITY (I11)

In the Italo-Flemish Renaissance style, its façade is that of a Temple of the Augustinians which used to be in the place de Brouckère.

THE OLD CHURCH OF THE BRIGITTINES(H7)

Built in the 17th century, abandonned since the 18th century. Restored in 1850, it was used for various purposes before becoming a cultural centre (open during cultural events).

THE PALACE OF THE NATION (J-K6)

It was built in 1783 for the Sovereign Council of Brabant. Originally the Palace of the States-General in 1817, it became the Palace of the Nation after 1830. Since then the Senate and the Chamber of Representatives have met whithin its walls.

THE CHURCH OF NOTRE-DAME DE LAEKEN

Constructed in the 19th century and dedicated to Louise-Marie, first queen of the Belgians, it contains the Royal Crypt. At the cemetery are burried a number of well-known personalities. Among the works of art decorating the tombs and chapels is the famous "Thinker", by Auguste Rodin.
Royal Crypt : access by avenue du Parc Royal.

THE "MONTS DES ARTS". (I 6)

Vast architectural complex of modern buildings in the centre of which reposes a beautiful public terraced garden. The "Monts-des-Arts" includes also the small St-George's Chapel, last vestige of the old Nassau Palace.
Also remarkable is "The Monumental Music Clock" animated by twelve statues seven feet high.

The **"Palais des Congrès"** whose well studied arrangement offers to business, cultural and political groups excellent facilities for all sorts of conventions, meetings and conferences; the **Albertine Library**, one of the richest in Europe (more than a million and a half books, 30.000 inestimable ancient manuscripts)

The **"Palais de la Dynastie"** where patriotic manifestations are held. At the lower end of the esplanade stands the equestrian monument of Albert I (Sculptor Courtens' masterpiece).

THE ATOMIUM (hors plan)

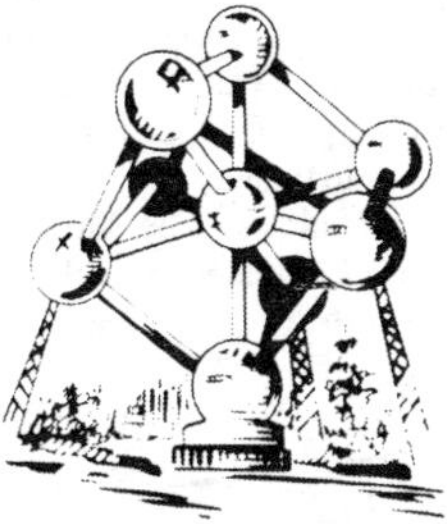

Impressive and lasting symbol of the 1958 Brussels' World Fair, the shining steel-and-aluminium atomium represents an iron molecule magnified 200 billion times. The upper sphere (height 330 feet) houses a panoramic restaurant. Scientific exhibitions are held in the side spheres.

THE "PARC DE BRUXELLES" AND THE "PALAIS DE LA NATION" (JK 6)

The park was formerly the hunting ground of the Dukes of Brabant. Since the 18th century, it has been converted into a well laid-out french garden decorated with statues and ponds.
In 1830 the park was the principal battlefield where the fight between the Dutch troops and the Belgian insurgents took place. At the northern part of the park the "Palais de la Nation" (Senate and House of Representatives) is situated.

THE "PETIT SABLON" SQUARE (I 8)

This beautiful little garden situated in front of the ogival Notre-Dame-des-Victoires church is surrounded by splendid wrought-iron railings. Forty-eight small columns delicately support statues representing the different mediaeval Corporations of the City. In the middle of the square stands the Egmont and Hornes' monument. (Two noblemen executed by the Spaniards in 1568). The upper part of the garden is lined by the Egmont's Palace, former residence of the Arenberg family. Louis XV, Voltaire, Queen Christina of Sweden and many others of European nobility sojourned in this palace.
A nice little park hidden behind this building offers an oasis of calm and tranquillity only a short distance away from the city's tumult.

THE "PALAIS DE JUSTICE" (Law Courts) (HI 8)

This colossal work of the architect Poelaert was built from 1866 to 1883 in a mixture of greek, roman and babylonian styles. The palace is the biggest european building of the 19th century. It contains 350 halls and a noteworthy antechamber. The cupola rises to a height of 340 feet. Even those who dislike the palace can't deny its majestic aspect and it is doubtless one of the most charecteristic elements of Brussels' landscape, certainly the most conspicuous.

THE BOURSE (The Stock Exchange) (H 6)

This temple of the Goddess "Finance" was built in 1871 in a composite neo-classic and Italian Renaissance style. The french sculptor Rodin participated in the façade's decoration. Impudent pigeons have chosen the building as their favorite home.

THE CONGRESS' COLUMN. (J 5)

Rising to the height of 154 feet, the column commemorates, since 1859, the National Congress that promulgated the Constitution of 1931. A statue of Leopold I, first king of the Belgians can be seen at the top. At the foot of the column rest two unknown soldiers of the World Wars. One has access to the top from which a worthwhile panorama of the city can be admired.

THE PLACE DES PALAIS. (Palaces' Square) (J 7)

The esplanade is bordered by the "Palais des Académies" (Academies' Palacc) thc Royal Palace and the Palace of Fine Arts. The **"Palais des Académies",** former residence of the Prince of Orange, was built from 1823 to 1826. It shelters, since 1876, the Belgian Royal Academy.

The **Royal Palace,** the most important of the buildings stretching along the square owes its present Louis XVI façade to King Leopold II who transformed the edifice in 1904.

The **"Palais des Beaux-Arts"** lays west of the square. It is a spacious building, built mostly underground by the architect V. Horta (1930). It contains many exhibition rooms, showrooms, a movie theatre and a great concert hall, famous for its acoustics.

THE "PLACE ROYALE" (Royal Square) (J 7)

This square, erected in the 18th century under the reign of Charles of Lorraine, is a beautiful example of classical and proportioned urbanism. In its middle stands the equestrian monument of Godefroid de Bouillon, first christian king of Jerusalem. Behind the statue stands the Saint Jacques-sur-Coudenberg Church which was used as a "Temple of the Reason" during the French Revolution.

THE CATHEDRALE SAINT-MICHEL (Saint-Michael's cathedral) (J 6)

Beautiful gothic edifice, synthesis of all the ogival art's periods from the 13th tot the 16th century.
The interior, simple and full of dignity receives light through splendid stained-glass windows some of which were designed by Bernard van Orley and given by the emperor Charles V of Habsbourg.
The pulpit, representing Adam and Eve's banishment from the earthly paradise, was carved in 1699.
Since the Middle Ages, the cathedral has witnessed some of the most historical events taking place in Brussels. The Dukes of Brabant, the Archdukes Albert and Isabelle and Charles of Lorraine are buried in the church.

THE ABBAYE DE LA CAMBRE (The Cambre Abbey)(L12)

The buildings of this ancient Cistercian abbey (founded at the end of the 13th century) are now surrounded by a charming terrace "French Garden". They shelter a well known Art Academy.
The simple and noble abbatial church was built in the 14th century. It is nevertheless perfectly integrated with the classic main buildings which were erected in the 17th century.
The National Geographic Institute is located in the buildings.

THE EGLISE NOTRE-DAME DE LA CHAPELLE (Notre-Dame of the Chapelle church)(H 7)

A very beautiful brabantine church overlooking the popular Marolles'borough. The romanic choir and the gothic transept date from the 13th century, the nave from the 15th. Peter Breughel the Ancient's grave is in one of the southern aisle's chapels.

PORTE DE HAL (The Hal Tower) (G 9)

This massive and impressive building is the last vestige of Brussels' second rampart. It was built in 1380 and restored in 1870. It now shelters the Royal Museum of Arms and Armours.

OPERA HOUSE THEATRE ROYAL DE LA MONNAIE (The Royal Mint Theater) (I 5)

The peristyle and the fronton's bas-relief are the last vestiges of the theatre that was originally built in 1817 and where the first dramatic events of the Belgian Revolution took place in 1830. The actual edifice dates back to 1885. It houses Belgium's most famous opera and the well known XXth Century Ballet.

THE NATIONAL HOLY HEART'S BASILICA (C 1)

This vast temple overlooking the western part of the city was begun in 1926. The cupola reaches a height of 327 feet.
The basilica's solemn consecration's ceremonies took place in 1951. From the central altar radiates 10 chapels dedicated to the 9 Belgian provinces and Zaire.

MANNEKEN-PIS FOUNTAIN(H 6)

This small bronze statuette (Dusquesnoy 1619) called "the oldest citizen of the city" represents a young hero from the Brussels' folklore. The Manneken-Pis owns a varied and abundant trousseau which is kept in the Communal Museum. It goes from a Japanese Samourai's armour to a Georgian dancer's costume.

WATERLOO (h. p.)

Renowned for the battle of the 18th June 1815 which in reality took place on the territory of the neigbouring communes. On the hillock, the "Lion" which faces towards France, was made from the bronze canons of Napoleon's army.

Sights to be seen :

The panorama - The wax museum - Historical farms (La Haie Sainte and Mont-St-Jean) (Hougoumont) - La ferme du Caillou (Napoleon's H.Q.) and Wellington's museum (Duke of Wellington's H.Q.).

Waterloo church contains various souvenirs of this epoch.

PRINCIPAL MUSEUMS

ROYAL MUSEUMS OF ART AND HISTORY (N7)

Avenue des Nerviens (Cinquantenaire), Tel. 741.72.11.

Even days : Egyptian, Greek and Roman antiquities Ancient Near-East, Pre-Columbian civilisations. American ethnography and archeology. Far-East art and ethnography. National Folklore.

Odd days : Industrial art : wood and stone sculpture, goldsmith art, tapestry, laces, ceramics, glass work, history of carriages.

ROYAL MUSEUMS OF FINE ARTS (I7)

Rue de la Régence 3, Tel. 508.32.11.
Painting - Ancient art. Consists mainly of the flemish school of XIV to XVIIth century. Breughel, Rubens, Van Dijck, etc....

MUSEUM OF MODERN ART (I7)

Pl. Royale 1-2, Tel. 508.32.11.
Paintings, drawings and sculptures of XIX and XX centuries. Principally French and Belgian schools.

ROYAL LIBRARY ALBERT Ier (I7)

General library : Bld. de l'Empereur 4, 1000 Bruxelles, Tel. 519.53.11.
Public entrance : Mont des Arts : open from 9 am to 9 pm.
Manuscripts Department : Splendid collection of manuscripts and illuminated books principally of the Burgundian period.
Medals and coins Department.

BRUSSELS MUNICIPAL MUSEUM (I6)

"Maison du Roi" Grand-Place,
Rue Poivre 1, Tel. 279.43.50.
History and archeology of the town. Tapestry, altarscreens, porcelain, faiences, lace and goldsmith art.

WIERTZ MUSEUM (L8)

Rue Vauthier 62, Tel. 648.17.18.
Studio of the romantic painter A. Wiertz. Contains the majority of his works.

MUSEUM OF THE DYNASTY (J7)

Place des Palais 7, Tel. 511.55.78.
Iconographic documents of the Belgian Royal Family from 1830 till now.

PUBLIC CITY TRANSPORT (h.p.)

Av. de Tervueren 364b, 1150 Bruxelles, Tel. 515.31.08.
Museum which retraces public city transport by means of vehicles of different Belgian transport companies and this from horse traction to electric tramcars.

ROYAL ARMY MUSEUM (O7)

Parc du Cinquantenaire 3, Tel. 733.44.93.
Military souvenirs from the end of the XVIIIth century, principally of the First World War.

BELGIAN ROYAL INSTITUTE OF NATURAL SCIENCES (L8)

Chaussée de Wavre 260, Tel. 627.42.11.
Sections covering : zoology, paleontology, mineralogy, paleobotany, anthropology and national prehistory.

AUTOMOBILE MUSEUM - AUTOWORLD (N8)

Parc du Cinquantenaire 11
1000 Bruxelles, Tel. 736.41.65.
500 vehicles trace the evolution of the automobile construction back to 1896.

MUSEUM OF CENTRAL AFRICA (h. p.)

Château de Tervuren, chaussée
de Louvain 13, 1980 Ter, Tel. 769.52.11.
Anthropology, prehistory, ethnography.
Geology, mineralogy, botanics, zoology.

POST AND TELECOMMUNICATIONS MUSEUM (I7)

Place du Grand Sablon 40, 1000 Bruxelles, Tel. 511.77.40.
Free entrance.
Belgian and foreign stamps, history of the postal services, evolution of telecommunication.

INSTRUMENTAL MUSEUM OF THE MUSIC CONSERVATORY (I8)

Place du Petit Sablon 17, Tel. 511.35.95
Musical instruments of all periods and countries, more than 150 unique pieces in the world.

LACE AND COSTUMEMUSEUM (I6)

Rue de la Violette 6, 1000 Br., Tel.512.77.09
The museum, situated behind the townhall, contains a rich collection of lace and costumes of the 17th century till nowadays. Exhibitions with changing themes.

BREWERY MUSEUM (I6)

Grand Place 10, 1000 Br., Tel.511.49.97
A beautiful collection of pewter pots and stoneware jugs, communal ordinances on the good use of beer and an authentic 17th century brewery.

MUSEUM CONSTANTIN MEUNIER (K12)

Rue de l'Abbaye 59, 1050 Br., Tel.648.44.49
Oil paintings, sculptures, water-colours and drawings of Constantin Meunier (1831-1905).

MUSEUM OF THE ROYAL INSTITUTE FOR NATURAL SCIENCES OF BELGIUM (L8)

Rue Vautier 29, 1050 Br., Tel.627.42.11
In a totally renewed museum, the visitor gets a good view on the richness of animal life on earth, now and in pre-history, by the means of diaramas and show cases. There also is an exhibition of minerals.

CHILDREN'S MUSEUM (LM12)

Rue du Bourgmèstre - 1050 Br. -
Tel. 640.01.07
Specially for children from 6 to 12 years.

WAX MUSEUM (HISTORIUM)(I5)

Anspachcenter - 1re étage
Bld. Anspach, 1000 Br., Tel. 217.60.23
Twenty scenes with life-size wax figures and approriate settings make a visit to this museum an unforgettable journey through 2000 years of the history of Belgium.

NUMISMATIC AND HISTORICAL MUSEUM OF THE BELGIAN NATIONAL BANK (J6)

Rue du Bois Sauvage 9, 1000 Br., Tel.507.83.70
Exhibition on the history of money.

CINEMA MUSEUM (J6)

Rue Baron Horta, 1000 Br.,
Tel. 513.41.55
Permanent exhibition and projection of old films.

HORTA MUSEUM (J11-12)

Rue Américaine 25 - 1060 Br. -
Tel. 537.16.92
Installed in the house of this famous architect.

AVIATION MUSEUM (O7)

Parc du Cinquantenaire 3 - 1000 Br. -
Tel. 733.44.93
More than a 130 planes of all types and times, of which 80 are exhibited. The museum gives, a complete survey of the history of civilian and military aviaton, the para-commandos, aerial photos, etc...

MUSEUM OF THE BRUSSELS SOCIAL SERVICES CENTRE (H8)

Hôpital Saint-Pierre, Rue Haute 298A, 1000 Br, Tel. 535.30.28

Paintings,sculptures, tapestries and furniture (15th - 18th century).

TOY MUSEUM (K5)

Rue de l'Association 24, 1000 Br,
Tel. 219.61.68

NATIONAL MUSEUM OF THE RESISTANCE(E7)

Rue Van Lint 14, 1070 Br.,
Tel. 522.40.41

JEWISH MUSEUM OF BELGIUM (G7)

Avenue de Stalingrad 24, 1000 Br.,
Tel. 512.19.63
Jewish customs and art in Belgium.

DAVID AND ALICE VAN BUUREN MUSEUM (h. p.)

Avenue L. Errera 41, 1180 Br.,
Tel. 343.48.51
Splendid collections of paintings from the 16th to the 20th century, including an outstanding version of "The fall of Icarus" painted by Bruegel the Elder.

CENTRE FOR HISTORY AND TRADITIONS OF THE GENDARMERIE (O11)

Avenue de la Force Aérienne 33, 1040 Br., Tel. 642.69.29

ERASMUS HOUSE (B8)

Rue du Chapitre 31, 1070 Br.,
Tel. 521.13.83
The prince of Humanists stayed here in 1521. The rooms are richly furnished and decorated. Remarkable collection of documents illustrating the life and work of Erasmus.

BELGIAN COMIC STRIP CENTRE (J6)

Rue de Sable 26, 1000 Br., Tel. 219.19.80
Installed in the former Waucquez stores (architect V. Horta, Art Nouveau). About the birth and evolution of the comic strip, and the history of about 60 years of the creation of comic strips in Belgium and Europe.
There is also a library with the largest comic strip collection in the world and there are organised temporary expositions and prestigous events.

STREETS	PARISH COUNCILS	PLAN
A		
Abattoir (bld. de l')	B	FG6
Abattoir (rue de l')	B	G6
Abbaye (rue de l')	XL	K12
Abbé de l'Epée (rue)	WL	R7
Abdication (rue de l')	B	N5
Abondance (rue de l')	SJ	KL4
Abricotier (rue de l')	B	H8
Acacias (place des)	Et	NO9
Accord (rue de l')	Mo	D4
Adriaens (rue Doyen)	Mo	G3
Aduatiques (rue des)	Et	PQ8
Aerschot (rue d')	Sc	J2-3
Africaine (rue)	SG	I11
Agora (Galeries)	B	I6
Agrafe (rue de l')	An	C7
Agrément (rue de l')	An	AB8
Agriculture (rue de l')	Sc	O1
Aiguille (rue de l')	An	C7-8
Ailes (rue des)	Sc	L1
Albanie (rue d')	SG	H11
Albert (avenue)	Fo	GH12
Albert (place)	Fo	G12
Albert (rue Prince)	XL	J9
Albert-Elisabeth (av.)	WL	PQ7
Albertin (av.)	WL	Q7
Albertine (place de l')	B	I6
Albert 1er (square)	An	D8
Alexiens (rue des)	B	H7
Allard (rue)	Sc	J3
Allard (rue Ernest)	B	I7-8
Allée Verte	B2	I1-2
Alliance (rue de l')	SJ	K5
Alliés (rue des)	Fo	E11-12
Alost (rue d')	B	G5
Alouettes (av. des)	WP	R11
Alsace-Lorraine (rue d')	XL	K8
Alsemberg (ch. d')	Fo-SG	G11-12
Amandiers (av. des)	Mo	A4
Amazone (rue de l')	XL-SG	IJ11
Ambiorix (square)	B	M6
Amblève (rue de l')	Au	P11
Américaine (rue)	XL-SG	J11-12

STREETS	PARISH COUNCILS	PLAN
Amigo (rue de l')	B	H6
Amitié (place de l')	Au	P11
Anciens Combat. (av. des)	Ev	R2-3
Andenne (rue d')	SG	G10
Anderlecht (porte d')	B	FG6
Anderlecht (rue d')	B	G6
Anglaise (rue)	Mo	G3
Angle (rue de l')	B2	I3
Angleterre (rue d')	SG	G8-9
Anneessens (place)	BG	7
Anneessens (rue)	B	G6
Anoul (rue)	XL	K8
Anspach (boulevard)	B	H5-6
Anvers (boulevard d')	B	HI3-4
Anvers (chaussée d')	B	I3
Anvers (porte d')	B	I4
Août (av. d')	WL	R6
Aqueduc (rue de l')	XL-SG	IJ11
Arbalétriers (rue des)	B	H7
Arbre (rue de l')	B	I8
Arbre Bénit (rue de l')	XL	J9
Arc (rue de l')	B2	I3
Archers (rue des)	Ko	E1
Archimède (rue)	B	M6-7
Ardenne (rue Jean d')	XL	J9
Arenbert (rue d')	B	I6
Argent (rue d')	B	I5
Argonne (rue de l')	SG	G8
Arlon (rue d')	B-XL	L7
Armateurs (pont et place des)	B2	HI2
Armateurs (quai des)	B2	I1
Armée (av. de l')	Et	P8-9
Armet (av. de l')	Ev	Q3
Armistice (rue de l')	Ko	E2
Arrosoir (rue de l')	B	G8
Artan (rue)	Sc	M3-4
Artémis (av.)	Ev	R2
Artichaut (rue de l')	SJ	L6
Artisans (rue des)	XL	M9
Artois (rue d')	B	G7
Arts (avenue des)	B	K6-7
Ascension (rue de l')	SJ	K3
Assaut (rue d')	B	I5

STREETS	PARISH COUNCILS	PLAN
Association (rue de l')	B	K5
Astronomie (av. de l')	SJ	K5
Ateliers (rue des)	Mo	G3
Athénée (rue de l')	XL	JK9
Atrébates (rue des)	Et	PQ8-9
Auber (avenue)	An	B8
Auderghem (av. d')	B-Et	N9
Augustins (rue des)	B	HI5
Aumale (rue d')	An	B8
Aurore (rue de l')	B	L12
Automne (rue de l')	XL	N12
Autonomie (rue de l')	An	F7
Autrique (rue Léon)	Ko	E3
Avenir (rue de l')	Mo	G4
Aviation (sq. de l')	An	G7
Avril (av. d')	WL	R5
Azalées (av. des)	Sc	MN3

● B ●

STREETS	PARISH COUNCILS	PLAN
Baeck (av. Joseph)	Mo	CD5
Bailli (rue du)	B-XL	J11
Balis (pl. Thomas)	Au	R12
Banning (rue Emile)	XL	M12
Banque (rue de la)	B	J5
Bara (place)	An-SG	F8
Bara (rue)	An	EF8-9
Barchon (rue de)	B	H4
Baron (rue Théodore)	Au	Q12
Barques (quai aux)	B	H4
Barricades (pl. des)	B	K5
Barrière de St.-Gilles	SG	G10
Barthélémy (bld.)	B	G5
Basilique (av. de la)	BA-Ko	A2-B1-2-C1
Basse (rue Frédéric)	B	G8
Bassin Beco	B2	H2-3
Bassin Vergote	B2	I1
Bassins (rue des)	An	D8
Bastion (rue des)	An	D8
Bastion (square du)	XL	J8
Bastogne (place de)	Ko	C2
Bataves (rue des)	Et	P8
Bateau (rue du)	Mo	E6

STREETS	PARISH COUNCILS	PLAN
Batelage (quai du)	B2	H3
Baucq (rue Philippe)	Et	MN9-10
Baudet (rue du)	B	J7-8
Baudouin (boulevard)	B	HI3-4
Béatitude (av. de la)	Ev	QR3
Beau Site (rue du)	B	J10
Beauté (place de la)	An	B7-8
Becker (r. Lt. Jérôme)	Et	O10
Beckers (rue)	Et	N10
Beeckman de Crayloo (rue)	An	A6
Beco (av. Emile de)	XL	M12
Beffroi (rue du)	B	N5-6
Béguinage (place du)	B	H5
Béguinage (rue du)	B	H4
Béguines (rue des)	Mo	AB3
Belgica (boulevard)	Mo	FG1
Belgrade (rue de)	Fo-SG	E10
Belle au Bois Dormant (rue de la)	Mo	A5
Belle Vue (rue de)	B-XL	L12
Belliard (rue)	B	KL7
Belvédère (rue du)	XL	L11
Bemel (rue du)	WP	R10
Benès (avenue Ed.)	Mo	B2
Benoit (rue Peter)	Et	N9
Béranger (rue)	Fo	E12
Berceau (rue du)	B	L6
Berchem (rue de)	Mo	F3
Berchem-Ste-Agathe (avenue de)	Ko	C2
Berckmans (rue)	SG	H19
Bergé (rue Henri)	Sc	L2
Berger (rue du)	XL	J8
Bergère (av. de la)	BA	B1
Bernheim (av. Gén.)	Et	N11
Bernier (avenue Gén.)	XL	L12
Bernier (rue Fern.)	Fo-SG	F10
Berthelot (rue)	Fo	E11
Bertrand (av. Louis)	Sc	LM2
Bertulot (rue André)	SJ	J4
Besace (rue de la)	B	N6
Besma (avenue)	Fo	FG12
Besme (rue Jules)	Ko	CD2
Bethège (rue Marcel)	Mo	D3

STREETS	PARISH COUNCILS	PLAN
Bethléem (place de)	SG	F10
Beudin (rue Dr. Ch.)	Mo	C3
Beughem (rue de)	Sc	K3
Beurre (rue au)	B	I6
Beyaert (rue Henri)	B	K6
Biarritz (square du)	XL	KL11
Bien-Etre (rue du)	An	B5
Bienfaisance (r. de la)	SJ	IJ3
Bienfaiteurs (pl. des)	Sc	MN3
Bigorne (rue de la)	SJ	L5
Billard (rue du)	Mo	G4-5
Binjé (rue Frans)	Sc	MN3
Biot (rue Gustave)	XL	M11-12
Birmingham (rue de)	An-Mo	C7-D5-E6
Bisschoffsheim (bld)	B	K5
Bissé (rue)	An	F7
Bivouac (rue du)	An	C6
Blaes (rue)	B	IGH8-9
Blanche (rue)	B-XL-SG	IJ10
Blanchisserie(rue de la)	B	IJ4
Blé d'Or (rue du)	BA	A3
Blindés (sq. des)	B	H4
Blyckaerts (pl. Raym.)	XL	L9
Bobine (impasse de la)	B	J5
Bocq (rue du)	Au	P11
Bodeghem (rue)	B	G7
Bodenbroeck (rue)	B	I7
Boduognat (rue)	B	M6
Boendael (ch. de)	XL	L11-M12
Boers (rue des)	Et	O8-9
Bogards (rue des)	B	H6
Boileau (avenue)	Et	Q9
Bois à Brûler (Quai au)	B	H4-5
Bois de Construction (quai au)	B	H4
Bois de Linthout (rue du)	WL	R6
Bois Sauvage (rue du)	B	J6
Boiteux (rue des)	B	I5
Bolivar (bld. Simon)	B	I2-3
Bollandistes (rue des)	Et	PQ9
Bon Accueil (rue du)	B	AB1
Bonehill (rue Edmond)	Mo	DE5
Bonne (rue de)	Mo	DE6

STREETS	PARISH COUNCILS	PLAN
Bonneels (rue)	SJ	M5
Bonnevie (rue)	Mo	F4
Bon Pasteur (rue du)	Mo	A3
Bons Secours (rue du)	B	H6
Bonté (rue de la)	B-SG	I9
Boone (rue Doyen)	Et	N8
Bordeaux (rue de)	SG	HI10
Bordiau (rue)	B	N5-6
Borgval	B	H6
Borgendael (rue)	B	J7
Borne (rue de la)	Mo	F4
Borrens (rue)	XL	L11
Bortier (Galerie)	B	I6
Bosnie (rue de)	SG	F10-11
Bosquet (rue)	SG	I9
Bossaert (avenue E.)	Ko	CD2
Bossaerts (rue Franç.)	Sc	N4
Bossu (rue Paul)	WP	Q9
Bossuet (place Fr.)	SJ	L4
Botanique (rue)	SJ	JK4
Bouchers (petite rue des)	B	I6
Bouchers (rue des)	B	I6
Bougie (rue de la)	An	F6
Bouillon (rue Jules)	XL	K9
Bougainvillea's (r. des)	Mo	A5
Bouillot (rue E.)	XL	I12
Boulet (rue du)	B	G5
Boulevard (av. du)	B	IJ4
Bouré (rue)	XL	K8-9
Bourg (rue Colonel)	Sc	PQ5
Bourgmestre (rue du)	XL	LM12
Bourse (place de la)	B	H5-6
Bourse (rue de la)	B	H6
Bouvier (rue)	Mo	H2
Bouvier (sq. Baron A.)	SG	I10
Bovie (rue Félix)	XL	L10-11
Brabançonne (av. de la)	B-Sc	N5
Brabant (rue de)	SJ-Sc	JK2-3
Braemt (rue)	SJ	L5
Braffort (r. Bâtonnier)	Et-WL	PQ7-8
Braie (rue de la)	B	G4-5
Brand (rue Joseph)	Sc	L1-2
Brand Whitlock (bld.)	WL-WP	Q7-8
Brasserie (av. de la)	An	F7

STREETS	PARISH COUNCILS	PLAN
Brasserie (rue de la)	XL	L10
Brasseurs (rue des)	B	I6
Brassine (av. Charles)	Au	P12
Braves (rue des)	Ko	E2
Bréart (rue Antoine)	Fo-SG	GH11
Bréderode (rue de)	B	J7
Bremet (pl. Colonel)	Sc	M4
Breughel (rue)	B	H9
Breydel (rue)	B	M7
Brialmont (rue)	S	JK4
Brichaut (rue)	Sc	K2
Brigittines (pet. r. des)	B	H7
Brigittines (rue des)	B	H7
Briques (quai aux)	B	H4-5
Britsiers (av. Urbain)	Sc	N1
Brochet (rue du)	XL	M9
Brodeurs (rue des) (Cité)	B	H8
Broeck (rue du)	An	A8
Broeren (rue J.)	An	B8
Brogniez (rue)	An	EF7-8
Bronze (rue du)	An	C8
Broustin (avenue)	Ga-JP	DE1
Broyère (rue)	An	F6
Bruges (rue de)	Mo	B3
Brugmann (av.)	Fo-SG-XL	HI12
Brunfaut (rue de)	Mo	F5
Brune (rue)	An	B8
Bruxelles (ch. de)	Fo	E12
Bruylants (rue)	Et	P9
Buanderie (rue de la)	B	G6
Buchholtz (rue)	XL	JK12
Buedts (rue Joseph)	Et	O10
Buisson (rue du)	B-XL	KL12
Buls (rue Charles)	B	I6
Buntincx (rue M.)	Au	R12
Buysse (rue C.)	An	A7

● C ●

STREETS	PARISH COUNCILS	PLAN
Cadran (rue du)	SJ	L4
Call et Halot (rue)	Mo	F5
Calliope (rue)	Mo	C4
Calvin (rue)	B	M5
Cambier (av. Ernest)	Sc	O3-4
Cambre (rue de la)	WP-WL	R8
Camélias (av. des)	WP	R10
Camions (rue des)	Sc	J2-3
Campanules (rue des)	Mo	D3
Campenhout (rue Arm.)	XL	J11
Campine (rue de la)	Mo	E4
Camusel (rue)	B	G6
Canada (rue du)	Fo	F11
Canal (rue du)	B	H4
Canaris (avenue des)	Au	R12
Candries (av. Edm.)	Mo	A3-B4
Canon (rue du)	B	J4-5
Cans (rue)	XL	K9
Cantersteen	B	I6
Capiaumont (rue Gén.)	Et	M9-10
Capouillet (rue)	SG	I9
Capricorne (av. du)	WL	R4
Caucines (av. des)	Sc	N2
Caoucins (rue des)	B	H8
Carabiniers (pl. des)	Sc	P5
Cardinal (rue du)	B-SJ	M5-6
Caroly (rue)	XL	K8
Caron (rue H.)	An	A7
Carpe (rue de la)	Mo	E4
Carpentier (rue Emile)	An	D8
Carrière (rue de la)	Ko	C2
Carrousel (rue du)	B	M5
Carton de Wiart (av.)	JP	EF1
Caserne (rue de la)	B	G7
Casernes (avenue des)	Et	N10
Cassiopée (av.)	WL	R5
Cassiopée (clos)	WL	R5
Castel (avenue du)	WL	QR7
Cattleyas (avenue des)	WP	Q11
Cattoir (rue Eug.)	XL	N12
Cavalerie (av. de la)	Et	N11
Cavatine (r. de la)	Mo-An	A5
Céleri (rue du)	SG	G10
Célidée (rue de la)	Mo	D3
Celtes (avenue des)	Et	O8
Cendres (rue des)	B	J4
Centenaire (av. du)	WL	R4-5
Centenaire (clos)	WL	R5

STREETS	PARISH COUNCILS	PLAN
Centre (galerie du)	B	I5-6
Cerisiers (av. des)	Sc	PQ5-6
César (avenue J.)	WP	R9
Chair et Pain (rue)	B	I6
Chaisiers (r.des) (Cité)	B	H8
Chalet (rue du)	SJ	L5
Chalon (rue Renier)	XL	J12
Chambéry (rue de)	Et	N10
Champ de Mars (p. du)	XL	J8
Champ de Mars (r. du)	B-XL	JK8
Champ d'Ossegem (r.)	Mo	B4
Champ du Roi (rue)	Et	NO9
Champs (avenue des)	Et	O10
Champs (rue des)	Et	NO10
Champs-Elysées (r.des)	XL	K10
Chancellerie (r. de la)	B	J6
Chandeliers (rue des)	B	I7
Chant d'Alouette (place du)	Mo	D4
Chant d'Oiseau (av. du)	Au-WP	QR11
Chanteurs (rue des)	B2	I3
Chantier (quai du)	B	H4
Chantier (rue du)	B	H4
Chapeau (rue du)	An	E7
Chapelain (rue du)	An	B8
Chapeliers (rue des)	B	I6
Chapelle (place de la)	B	H7
Chapelle (rue de la)	B	H7
Chapitre (rue du)	An	B8
Char (rue du)	B	G5
Charbo (avenue)	Sc	N5
Charbonnages(quai des)	Mo	G3-4
Charbonniers (rue des)	SJ	IJ3
Charcot (rue Com.)	An	B7
Chardons (rue des)	Sc	O3-4
Charité (rue de la)	B-SJ	K5-6
Charlemagne (bld.)	B	M6-7
Charleroi (ch. de)	B-SG	I9-10-11
Charles-Quint (av.)	Ba-Ga	BC1
Charles-Quint (rue)	B	MN5
Charles VI (rue)	SJ	L5
Charme (rue du)	Fo	E12
Charpentiers (rue des) (Cité)	B	H8
Chartreux (rue des)	B	GH5
Chasse (avenue de la)	Et	NO9

STREETS	PARISH COUNCILS	PLAN
Chasse Royale (r.de la)	Au	P12
Chasseur (rue du)	B	H7
Chasseurs Ardennais (place des)	Sc	N5
Château (av. du)	Ko	B1-C2
Château (rue du)	XL	M10
Châtelain (place du)	XL	J11
Châtelain (rue du)	B-XL	J11
Chaufferette (rue de la)	B	H6
Chaumière (rue de la)	Sc	K3
Chaux (quai à la)	B	H4
Chazal (avenue)	Sc	N3-4
Chemin de Fer (rue du)	SJ	J4
Chêne (rue du)	B	H6
Chevalerie (av. de la)	B	O7-8
Chevaliers (rue des)	XL	J8
Cheval Noir (rue du)	Mo	G4-5
Chevauchée (av. de la)	Ev	Q3
Chevreuil (rue du)	B	H8
Chien Marin (rue du)	B	H5
Chien Vert (rue du)	Mo	G4
Chimiste (rue du)	An	F6
Chœur (rue du)	Mo	G3
Chomé (rue Henri)	Sc	P3-4
Chomé-Wijns (rue)	An	D8
Choux (rue aux)	B	J5
Christine (rue)	B	HI8
Christophe (rue)	BA	A1
Cible (rue de la)	Sc-SJ	M5
Cigogne (rue de la)	B	G4-5
Cimetière (av. du)	Ev	R2-3
Cimetière de St.-Josse-ten-Noode	Sc	P3
Cinéma (rue)	Mo	F4
Cirque (rue du)	B	I4
Cité	B	H8
Cité Administrative	B	J5
Cité (rue de la)	XL	K9
Cité de la Chaussée	B	M7
Cité Fontainas	SG	G9
Cité Moderne(rue de la)	BA	B1
Cité Sotteau	Mo	DE3
Cité Terdelt	Ev	OP1
Cité Verte	Sc	P2
Claes (rue Caporal)	Sc	N1

STREETS	PARISH COUNCILS	PLAN
Claes (rue Joseph)	SG	FG9
Claeys (avenue)	Sc	MN4
Clef (rue de la)	B	G4-5
Clémenceau (av. G.)	An	F7
Clémentine (avenue)	Fo-SG	F11
Clémentine (rue)	XL	L9
Clinique (rue de la)	An	F7
Clocher (rue du)	Et	N8
Cloître (allée du)	B	L12
Clos (avenue des)	Sc	P3
Clos des Fleurs	Sc	P3
Clos des Mouettes	Sc	P2
Clos du Mouron	WP	R10
Clos de l'Oasis	Ev	P2
Clos des Poètes	Sc	P3
Clos Victor Gilsoul	WL	R7
Clovis (boulevard)	B	M5
Cluysenaar (r. Alfred)	SG	G11
Cocq (pl. Fernand)	XL	K9
Coenen (rue Louis)	SG	GH10
Coenraets (rue)	SG	F9
Cogghe (rue l'Eclusier)	B2	J1
Colibri (rue du)	Mo	BC5
Colignon (place)	Sc	L1
Collecteur (rue du)	An	D8
Collège (rue du)	XL	K9-L10
Collège St.-Michel (rue du)	WP	QR9
Collégiale (rue de la)	B	J6
Colleye (rue)	Mo	F5
Colline (rue de la)	B	I6
Colombier (rue du)	B	I5
Colonies (rue des)	B	J6
Colonne (rue de la)	Mo	F4
Colzas (allée des)	Au	R12
Combattants (rue des)	BA	A1
Combaz (rue Gisbert)	SG	G10-11
Comédiens (rue des)	B	IJ5
Comète (rue de la)	SJ	K4
Comhaire (avenue R.)	BA	A2
Comines (rue de)	B	M7
Commerçants (r. des)	B	HI4
Commerce (galerie du)	B	I5
Commerce (quai du)	B	H3-4
Commerce (rue du)	B	K6-7

STREETS	PARISH COUNCILS	PLAN
Communale (place)	Mo	G4
Commune (rue de la)	SJ	L5
Compagnons (r. des)	Sc	P4
Compas (rue du)	An	E6-7
Comptoir (rue du)	Ko	C1-2
Comte de Flandre (rue du)	Mo	G4
Conciliation (rue de la)	An	B8
Concorde (rue de la)	B-XL	J9
Condor (av. du)	Mo	AB4-5
Confédérés (rue des)	B	N6
Confiance (rue de la)	Et	M9
Congrès (place du)	B	J5
Congrès (rue du)	B	K5
Conscience (av. Henri)	Ev	K10
Conscience (pl. Henri)	XL	K10
Conseil (pl. du)	An	E8
Conseil (rue du)	XL	K9
Consolation (r. de la)	Sc	LM4
Constellation (av. des)	WL	R5
Constitution (av. de la)	Ga	D1
Constitution (pl. de la)	SG	G8
Constitution (rue de la)	Sc	K3
Constructeur (rue du)	An	D7
Coopérateurs(place des)	BA	A1
Coopman (rue Théo)	Sc	O1
Coosemans(rue Joseph)	Sc	N4
Coppens (rue)	B	I7-8
Coquelicots (rue des)	Et	O9
Coquihat (rue)	Et	O10
Cordialité (r. de la)	An	B5
Cordier (av. Dr. Edm.)	Au	R12
Corhay (rue Louis)	Mo	B3
Cornet (rue du)	Et	N8
Cornet de Grez (rue)	SJ-Sc	K3
Cortenbergh (av. de)	B	NO6
Cosaques de la Meuse (avenue des)	Et	O10-11
Coteaux (rue des)	Sc	L3-4
Coude (rue du)	B	J6
Coudenberg (rue)	B	IJ7
Couloir (rue du)	XL	K10
Couronne (av. de la)	XL	LMN9-10-11-12
Couronnement (av. du)	WL	R7

STREETS	PARISH COUNCILS	PLAN
Court (rue Antoine)	Ko	E3
Courtens (av. Frans)	Sc	P3
Courtois (petite rue)	Mo	G3
Courtois (rue)	Mo	G3
Courtoisie (rue de la)	An	A5-6
Courtrai (rue de)	Mo	EF4
Couvent (rue du)	XL	K10
Crèche (rue de la)	XL	K9
Crespel (rue Cap.)	XL	I8-9
Creuse (rue)	Sc	L2
Crickx (rue)	SG	FG10
Crickx (rue Lt. Lamb.)	An	F7
Crocus (rue des)	An	A7
Croisades (rue des)	SJ	I4
Croissant (rue du)	Fo-SG	E10-F11
Croix (rue de la)	XL	JK9-10
Croix de Fer (rue de la)	B	K5-6
Croix de Pierre (r.de la)	SG	H10
Croix du Sud (av. de la)	WL	R5
Croix Rouge (sq. de la)	XL	L12
Cubisme (rue du)	Ko	E3
Cuerens (rue)	B	G6
Cuissez (rue Léon)	XL	M11
Cultes (rue des)	B	K5
Cultivateurs (rue des)	Et	O9-10
Cureghem (rue de)	B	G6
Cuve (rue de la)	XL	L10
Cuylits (rue Abbé)	An	F6
Cuypers (rue Abbé)	Et	P8
Cygnes (rue des)	XL	L10
Cyprès (rue du)	B	H5

• D •

STREETS	PARISH COUNCILS	PLAN
D'Accolay (rue)	B	H7
Dailly (avenue)	Sc	MN4
Dailly (place)	Sc	N5
Dalechamp (av. Robert)	WL	R5-6
Dam (rue du)	B	G6
Damien (rue Père)	Ev	P1
Damier (rue du)	B	I4-5
Dandoy (pl. Aimé)	Et	O10
Danemark (rue du)	SG	F9
Dansaert (r. Antoine)	B	GH5
D'Ardenne (rue Jean)	XL	J9
Darimont (rue)	Mo	G4
Daring (avenue du)	Mo	BC4
D'Aumale (rue)	An	B8
Dauphins (rue des)	Mo	B4
Dautzenberg (rue)	B-XL	K10-11
Debatty (avenue L.)	An	C6
De Becker (r. Jules)	Ko	E2
De Beco (av. Emile)	XL	M12
De Bériot (rue)	SJ	K5
De Berlaimont (bld.)	B	J5
De Boeck (r. August)	Ev	OP1
De Braeckeleer (r. H.)	Et	P7
De Broqueville (av.)	WL-WP	QR7-8
De Brouckère (place)	B	I5
De Brouchoven de Bergeyck (rue Jean)	B	J5
De Bruyn (rue)	SJ	L5
De Bruyne (rue Serg.)	An	EF7
Debuck (rue Charles)	Et	Q9
De Burlet (sq. J.)	Et	P7
De Castro (rue Baron)	Et	Q10
Décembre (rue de)	WL	R6
De Cock (pl. J.B.)	Mo	E5
De Cock (r. J.B.)	Mo	D4-E4-5
Decoster (r. Charles)	XL	K10
Decoster (rue Pierre)	Fo	E11
De Craene (r. Alex)	Sc	O1
De Crayer (rue)	B	K12
Decroly (square)	Mo	A4
De Deken (rue Père)	Et	P8-9
De Facqz (rue)	B-SG-XL	J10-I11
De Fiennes (rue)	An	F8
De Fierlant (rue)	Fo	E11
Defnet (rue Gust.)	SG	F10
De Gaulle (av. Gn.)	XL	L11-12
De Gerlache (rue)	Et	MN10
Degouve de Nuncques (rue W.)	Sc	Q5-6
D'Egmont (rue)	B	K8
Degorge (rue Eug.)	Mo	D4
Degreef (rue F.)	Sc	L2
De Greef (sq. J.B.)	Au	Q12
De Grimberghe		

STREETS	PARISH COUNCILS	PLAN
(rue Edm.)	Mo	F4
De Gronckel (rue Ch.)	Mo	A4
De Groux (rue Ch.)	Et	P7
De Gunst (rue Louis)	Mo	D5
De Haerne (rue)	Et	MN10
De Hennin (rue)	XL	K10
De Hornes (rue)	BJ	K8
De Jaer (av. Paul)	SG	G11
De Jamblinne de Meux (place)	Sc	O6
De Joncker (rue)	SG	I9
Deken (rue Père de)	Et	P8-9
Dekens (rue)	Et	N8
Dekeyn (rue Jos.)	SJ	M5
De Koninck (rue)	Mo	C4
Delacroix (r. Léon)	An	DE6
De la Hoese (av. J.)	Mo	C3
De Lalaing (rue Jacq.)	B	L7
Delantsheer (rue Léon)	Et	OP7
De Latour (rue Albert)	Sc	M4
Delaunoy (rue)	Mo	EF5
Delcoigne (rue Fr.)	Ko	F3
Delcourt (rue E.)	An	B8
Delhaize (rue Jules)	Mo	D3-4
Delhasse (rue Félix)	SG	H12
Delhaye (rue J.)	Au	Q12
Delhaye (square F.)	SJ	M5
Delhove (rue Louis)	Ga	C1
De Ligne (rue)	B	J5
Délivrance (sq. de la)	Fo	G12
De Locht (rue)	Sc	KL2
De Longueville (avenue Général)	WP	R9-10
Delporte (pl. Ant.)	SG	H11-12
Delporte (rue Aug.)	XL	M11
De Meersman (av. Ev.)	BA	A3
De Meersman (r. Dr.)	An	F7
De Meeus (sq.)	B-XL	K7-8
Déménageurs (rue des)	Mo	F4
De Mérode (rue)	Fo-SG	F9-G8
De Mérode (sq. Pr. J.)	Et	P8
De Messemaeker (rue P.J.)	Mo	D4
Demets (quai Fern.)	An	C7-D6
Demeur (av. Adolphe)	SG	H11

STREETS	PARISH COUNCILS	PLAN
Demol (rue Willem)	B2	I2
De Moranville (rue)	JP	EF1
Démosthène (rue)	An	B7
Demot (rue J.A.)	Et	M8
De Muylder (rue Guill.)	Au	Q12
De Nayer (rue S.)	An	C6
De Neck (rue)	Ko	E2
De Neuter (rue Arm.)	BA	A3
Denis (rue Hector)	XL	J12
Depaepe (rue César)	SG	G9
De Pascale (rue)	B	L7
De Potter (rue)	Sc	K2
De Ribaucourt (rue)	Mo	G2-3
De Roo (rue A.)	Sc	N1
De Roover (r. Emile)	Ko	C2
De Roovere (avenue)	Mo	D5
De Rudder (rue)	Mo	CD3
De Saegher (r. Henri)	Mo	E4-5
De Saulnier (r. Arm.)	Mo	B3-4
Deschampheleer (rue)	Mo	F3
Deschanel (av. Paul)	Sc	M2-3-4
Désirs (av. des)	Ev	R3
Desmet (pl. Henri)	An	C5
Desmet (rue Dés.)	Sc	O1
De Stassart (rue)	XL	J8-9
Destouvelles (rue)	B2-Sc	J1
Destrée (rue Jules)	Sc	O1
Destrier (av. du)	Ev	Q3
De Swaef (rue Léop.)	An	BC6
De Theux (rue)	Et	M9-10
De Thibault (av. Ed.)	Et	O9
Dethy (rue)	SG	G10
Deux-Eglises (rue des)	B-SJ	L5-6
Deux Gares (rue des)	An	DE9
Deux Maisons (rue des)	Ev	R2-3
Deuxième Régiment de Lanciers (av. du)	Et	NO11
Deux Ponts (rue des)	XL	L9
Deux Tilleuls (av. des)	WL	P7-8
Deux Tours (rue des)	SJ	LM5
Devaux (rue Paul)	B	H5
Devigne (rue Paul)	Sc	NO3
De Vinci (rue Léonard)	B	N6-7
Devoir (rue du)	An	B8
Devos (rue Jef)	Fo	E11

STREETS	PARISH COUNCILS	PLAN
Devreese (rue God.)	Sc	M3
Devroye (rue Père E.)	Et-WP	QR9
De Witte (rue Alph.)	XL	L11
De Witte de Haelen (r.)	B	G4
De Wynants (rue)	B	H8
Dhanis (rue Baron)	Et	OP10
D'Hoogvorst (rue)	Sc	JK2
Diamant (avenue du)	Sc	OP5
Diderich (rue Arth.)	SG	G11-12
Dietrich (av. H.)	WL	Q8
Digue (rue de la)	XL	L10
Dilbeek (rue de)	Mo	BC5
Dillens (pl. Julien)	SG	H9
Dillens (rue)	XL	L10
Dillie (rue Albert)	Ko	E2-3
Dinant (place de)	B	H7
Dinant (rue de)	B	H7
Diongre (rue J.)	Mo	B3
Discaille (rue Ernest)	Sc	L2
Dixmude (bld. de)	B	H3-4
Dix-Sept Avril (rue du)	Ev	R3
Dominicains (rue des)	B	I5-6
D'Oultremont (rue)	Et	P7
Douvres (rue de)	An	C8
Douze Apôtres (r. des)	B	J6
Doyen (rue Nicolas)	Mo	D6
Dragon (clos du)	W	LR5
Drapeau (rue du)	An	B8
Drapiers (rue des)	XL	J9
Droit (place du)	An	B8
Dryepondt (rue Dr.)	Et	N10
Dublin (rue de)	XL	K8
Dubois (rue Alfred)	Mo	C4
Dubois Thorn (rue)	Mo	D4
Dubreucq (rue major René)	XL	K8
Dubrucq (av. Jean)	Mo	F1-2-G1
Duc (rue du)	WP	QR8
Ducale (rue)	B	JK6-7
Duchesse (rue de la)	Et-WP	Q8
Duchesse de Brabant (place de la)	Mo	E5
Duc Jean (av. du)	Ga	D1
Ducpétiaux (avenue)	SG	G12-H11

STREETS	PARISH COUNCILS	PLAN
Dujardin (rue Joseph)	An	D8
Dumonceau (rue)	B	H9
Dumont (pl. Herm.)	SG	I10
Dunant (avenue H.)	Ev	Q3
Duployé (sq. Emile)	Sc	M3
Dupont (rue)	Sc	JK3
Dupont (rue Joseph)	B	I8
Dupont (rue Pierre)	Ev	PQ1
Dupuis (bld. Sylvain)	An	A8
Duquesnoy (rue)	B	I6
Duray (av. Emile)	XL	L12
Duydelle (rue)	Mo	C4
Dyle (rue de la)	B2	HI2

● E ●

STREETS	PARISH COUNCILS	PLAN
Ebats (rue des)	BA	A1
Eburons (rue des)	B	M6
Echelles (rue des)	B	I4
Echevins (rue des)	XL	L11-12
Eclipse (rue de l')	B	H6
Ecole (rue de l')	Mo	F4
Ecole Moderne (r. de l')	An	DE8
Economie (rue de l')	B	G8
Ecosse (rue d')	SG	HI9
Ecu (av. de l')	Ev	Q3
Ecuelle (rue de l')	B	N6
Ecuyer (rue de l')	B	I5
Eden City	Fo	E12
Edimbourg (rue d')	XL	J8
Edison (rue)	Fo	E11
Eeckelaers (rue)	SJ	M5
Eenens (rue Général)	Sc	LM1
Egalité (rue de l')	Et	N10
Eglantines (av. des)	WP	R10-11
Eglise Sainte-Anne (rue de l')	Ko	EF3
Eglise Saint-Gilles (rue de l')	SG	G9-10
Eglise Saint-Julien (avenue de l')	Au	Q12
Eisenhower (av. Gén.)	Sc	MN3
Electricité (rue de l')	An	D8
Elégie (rue de l')	Mo	BC4

STREETS	PARISH COUNCILS	PLAN
Eléonore (avenue)	WP	Q10-11
Eléphant (rue de l')	Mo	F4-5
Elise (rue)	XL	MN12
Eloy (rue)	An	E8
Emeraude (av. de l')	Sc	OP5
Empereur (bld. de l')	B	I6-7
Emulation (rue de l')	An	C7
Enclume (rue de l')	SJ	L5
Enfance Joyeuse (rue de l')	Mo	C4
Enghien (rue d')	Mo	D5-6
Enseignement (r. de l')	B	JK5
Ensor (rue James)	An	C7
Entr'aide (avenue de l')	BA	B1
Epargne (rue de l')	B	I4
Epée (rue de l')	B	H8
Eperonniers (impasse) (r.d. Eperonniers 27)	B	I6
Eperonniers (rue des)	B	I6
Eperons d'Or (av. des)	XL	L11
Eperviers (av. des)	WP	R11
Equinoxe (av. de l')	WL	R6
Erables (rue des)	ET	N9
Erasme (rue)	An	B8
Ermitage (rue de l')	XL	K10
Escadron (rue de l')	Et	P9
Escalier (rue de l')	B	I7
Escaut (rue de l')	Mo	G1
Escrimeurs (rue des)	B	H7-8
Espagne (place d')	B	I6
Espagne (rue d')	SG	HI11
Espérance (rue de l')	Mo	G3
Esplanade (rue de l')	B-XL	K8
Est (rue de l')	Ev	PQ2
Est (rue de l')	Sc	L2
Etang (rue de l')	Et	M9
Etangs (clos des)	Et	M8-9
Etangs d'Ixelles	XL	L11-12
Etangs Noirs (pl. des)	Mo	F3
Etangs Noirs (rue des)	Mo	E4
Eté (rue de l')	XL	N12
Etendard (rue de l')	B	N6
Eternité (av. de l')	An	B7
Etterbeek (ch. d')	B-Et	M7-8
Etudiants (rue des)	SG	H10

STREETS	PARISH COUNCILS	PLAN
Etuve (rue de l')	B	H6
Europe (bld. de l')	SG	FG8
Europe (carref. de l')	B	I6
Europe (sq. de l')	WP	Q10
Euterpe (rue)	Mo	C4
Evenepoel (rue H.)	Sc	P4
Eventail (rue de l')	B	H8
Evêque (rue de l')	B	H5
Evers (rue)	B	H9
Evolution (rue de l')	BA	A1
Expansion (rue de l')	An	B7

● F ●

STREETS	PARISH COUNCILS	PLAN
Fabriques (rue des)	B	G5
Facteur (rue du)	Mo	FG4
Faider (rue)	XL-SG	I10-J10-11
Faisans (rue des)	B	H9
Faubourg (rue des)	B	H9
Faubourg (rue du)	B2	I3
Fauchille (rue André)	WP	Q8-9
Faucon (rue du)	B	H8
Fauré (av. Gabriel)	Fo	F12
Ferme (rue de la)	SJ	L5
Féron (rue Emile)	SG	F9
Fétis (rue)	Et	N9
Février (av. de)	WL	QR5
Fiancée (rue de la)	B	I4
Fiennes (rue de)	B	EF8
Fierens (rue Doyen)	Mo	G3
Fierlant (rue de)	Fo	E11
Fiers (rue Edouard)	Sc	M2
Filature (rue de la)	SG	GH4
Filleul (rue du)	Fo	G12
Fin (rue)	Mo	F4
Finistère (rue du)	B	I4-5
Fivé (rue Général)	Et	O10
Flagey (pl. Eug.)	XL	KL10
Flandre (porte de)	B-Mo	G4
Flandre (rue de)	B	GH4-5
Flandre (rue du comte)	Mo	G4
Fléau d'Armes (av. du)	Ev	Q3
Flèche (rue de la)	B2	I3

STREETS	PARISH COUNCILS	PLAN
Flessingue (rue de)	Mo	F2
Fleuristes (rue des)	B	G8
Fleurs (rue aux)	B	I4-5
Fleurus (rue de)	XL	K8
Flins (allée de)	An	D7
Florence (rue de)	B-XL	IJ10
Floris (rue)	Sc	L1
Foch (av. Maréchal)	Sc	KL1
Foin (quai au)	B	H4
Fondation (rue de la)	BA	B1
Fonderie (rue de la)	Mo	F4
Fonsny (avenue)	Fo-SG	F9
Fonainas (place)	B	H6
Fontainas (rue)	SG	G9
Fontaine (rue de la)	B	G7
Fontaine d'Amour (r.)	Sc	M3
Foppens (rue)	An	F6
Forest (ch. de)	Fo-SG	F11-G9
Forestière (rue)	XL	J11-12
Forêt d'Houthulst (rue de la)	B	H4
Forge (rue de la)	SG	GH9
Fort (rue du)	SG	G10
Fort de Boncelles (r.du)	Et	P9
Fortifications (rue des)	SG	G10
Fortin (avenue F.)	Sc	P4
Fossé-aux-Loups (rue du)	B	I5
Foucart (av. Raym.)	Sc	O1
Foulons (rue des)	B	G7
Fourche (rue de la)	B	I5-6
Fourez (rue Léon)	Ko	F2
Fourmois (rue)	XL	I11-12
Foyer des Orphelins (rue du)	Mo	A4
Fraîcheur (rue de la)	Mo	C4
Fraiteur (pl. Arnaud)	Sc	P4
Francart (rue)	XL	J8
France (rue de)	An-SG	F8-9
Franck (rue César)	XL	N12
Francqui (rue Jules)	Fo	F11
Francs (rue des)	Et	OP8
Franklin (rue)	B	N6
Fraternité (rue de la)	Sc	JK3
Frédéric (rue L.)	Sc	O5
Frère-Orban (square)	B	KL7

STREETS	PARISH COUNCILS	PLAN
Frick (sq. Henri)	SJ	K5
Fripiers (rue des)	B	I5
Frissen (av. Thomas)	Au	Q11
Froebel (rue)	B	G6
Froissart (rue)	B-Et	M7-8
Front (avenue du)	Et	P9
Frontispice (rue du)	B2	I3
Fuchsias (rue des)	Mo	D2-3
Fulton (rue)	B	N6
Fuss (rue Gustave)	Sc	M4

● G ●

STREETS	PARISH COUNCILS	PLAN
Gachard (rue)	B-XL	K10-11
Gaillard (rue Frans)	SG	G10
Galilée (avenue)	B	K4-5
Galopin (av. Alex)	Et	O9
Gand (chaussée de)	Ba-Ko-Mo	A2-BCD3
Ganshoren (rue de)	BA	B1
Ganshoren (rue de)	Ko	E3
Gare (rue de la)	Et	P8
Garibaldi (rue)	Fo-SG	G11
Gassée (rue Pierre)	Mo	G1
Gaucheret (place)	Sc	J2
Gaucheret (rue)	Sc	J1
Gaulois (avenue des)	Et	O8
Gautier (rue Antoine)	Et	N9
Gay (rue F.)	WP	R8
Geefs (rue)	Sc	L3
Gémaux (av. des)	WL	R5
Gendebien (rue)	Sc	J2
Geneffe (r. de) (imp.)	Mo	F4
Gênes (rue de)	Fo	E10
Genève (rue)	Sc	PQ3
Genot (rue Joseph)	Mo-BA	AB2
Gentilhomme (rue du)	B	J6
Géomètre (rue du)	Mo	B4
George dit Marchal (r.)	Ko	E3
Georgin Jacques (av.)	Ev	R3-4
Gérance (rue de la)	Ba	A1
Géraniums (av. des)	WP	R10
Gérard (rue)	Et	OP7
Germoir (rue du)	XL	M10

STREETS	PARISH COUNCILS	PLAN
Gevaert (rue Aug.)	An	E8
Gheude (rue)	An	F7
Giele (avenue)	JP	E1
Gilisquet (av. Charles)	Sc	O2
Gille (av. Norbert)	An	C6-7
Gillon (rue)	SJ	K4
Gilsoul (av. Victor)	WL	R7
Gineste (rue)	SJ	J4
Giron (rue Alfred)	XL	LM10
Gisseleire Versé (av.)	BA	A2-3
Glacière (rue de la)	SG	H11-12
Glands (rue des)	Fo	E12
Glasgow (rue de)	An	C6-7
Glibert (rue)	B2	J2
Gloires Nationales (avenue des)	Ga-Ko	CDE1
Glycines (av. des)	Sc	N1
Godaux (av. Eug.)	Et-WP	Q9-10
Godecharle (rue)	XL	O8
Godefroid de Bouillon (rue)	SJ	K4
Goffart (rue)	XL	KL9
Goffin (avenue Josse)	BA	AB1
Goossens (rue)	Sc	L1
Gorges Bleues (av. des)	Au-WP	R11
Gosselles (rue de)	Mo	F6
Goujons (rue des)	An	D8
Gouttière (rue de la)	B	H6
Gouvernement Provisoire (rue du)	B	K5
Graindor (bld. Jules)	An	C6
Grand Air (rue du)	BA	B1
Grand-Bigard (rue de)	BA	A3
Grand-Cerf (rue du)	B	I8
Grand Duc (rue du)	Et	M9
Grande Haie (rue de la)	Et	P9
Grande-Ile (rue de la)	B	H6
Grande-rue-au-Bois	Sc	N4
Grand-Hospice (r. du)	B	H4
Grand-Place	B	I6
Grand-Pré (rue du)	BA	A3
Grands-Carmes (r.d.)	B	H6
Grand Serment (rue du)	B	G5
Gratry (rue Général)	Sc	P6
Gravelines (rue de)	B	M5

STREETS	PARISH COUNCILS	PLAN
Gray (rue)	Et-XL	LM9
Greffe (rue du)	An	B8
Grétry (rue)	B	H1-5
Greyson (rue Victor)	XL	L11-12
Gribaumont (av. Louis)	WL-WP	R7-8
Grisar (rue)	An	F8
Groeninghe (rue de)	Mo	E4
Grosjean Léon (av.)	Ev	R3-4
Grosse-Tour (rue de la)	B-XL	J9
Grüner (rue Marcel)	Mo	C3
Gueux (place des)	B	N6
Guffens (rue God.)	Sc	O1-2
Guillaume Franz (av.)	Ev	R2
Guidon (rue Fik)	Mo-BA	A3
Guildes (rue des)	B-SJ	L5-6
Guimard (rue)	B	K7
Gulden Bodem (rue du)	Mo	CD4
Gutenberg (square)	B	L6

● H ●

STREETS	PARISH COUNCILS	PLAN
Haberman (rue)	An	F6
Haecht (ch. de)	Sc-Sj	K3-L1-L2-M1
Haeck (rue)	Mo	F2
Haerne (rue)	Et	M9-10
Hainaut (quai du)	Mo	FG5
Hainaut (rue Auguste)	JP	FG5
Hal (porte de)	B	G9
Hallebarde (av. de la)	Ev	Q3
Hancart (rue)	Sc	L2
Hansen-Soulie (av.)	Et	P10
Hanssens (av. J.)	Mo	G2
Hanssens (rue Charles)	B	I8
Hap (rue Félix)	Et	N8
Hap (rue Louis)	Et	MN9
Hap-Lemaître (rue P.)	Et	N11
Harengs (rue des)	B	I6
Harmonie (rue de l')	B2	I3
Harnois (av. du)	Ev	Q3
Haubrechts (imp.)	Mo	G4
Haut-Champ (av. du)	BA	A3
Haute (rue)	B	H7-8-9
Haut-Pont (av. du)	XL-SG	I12

STREETS	PARISH COUNCILS	PLAN
Haut-Pont (carré du)	XL	J12
Havaux (rue E.)	Et	M9
Hectolitre (rue de l')	B	G8
Héger-Bordet (rue)	B	H9
Hélène (avenue)	BA	A2
Héliotropes (av. des)	Sc	N2
Héliport	B2	HI3
Héliport (av. de l')	B	I2
Hellinckx (rue Alph.)	Ga	C1
Hellinckx (rue Fr.)	Ko	E3
Helmet (chaussée de)	Sc	M1
Hennebicq (rue A.)	Fo-SG	F10
Hennin (rue de)	XL	K10
Henrard (rue Ed.-Ch.)	Au	Q11
Henri (av. Georges)	WL	PQR6-7
Henry (rue Général)	Et	O10
Herbette (bld. Maurice)	An	B6-7
Héris (rue)	B	G6
Herkoliers (rue)	Ko	F2-3
Herman (rue)	Sc	L2
Héros (place des)	SG	G9
Herreweghe (rue)	JP	E1
Heydenberg (av.)	WL	R5-6
Heymans (rue Hub.)	BA	A1
Heyvaert (rue)	An-Mo	EF6
Hiel (rue Emmanuel)	Sc	L1
Hippocampes (rue des)	Mo	B4
Hippodrome (av. de l')	XL	L12
Hirondelles (rue des)	B	I5
Hobbema (rue)	B	O6-7
Hoese (av. Jean de la)	Mo	C3
Hollande (rue de)	SG	G9
Hollevoet (av. H.)	Mo	F1-2
Homme-Chrétien (rue de l')	B	I6
Hoover Herbert (av.)	Sc	Q5-6
Hôpital (rue de l')	BI	6-7
Hôpital Français (avenue de l')	Ko	BC1
Horizon (av. de l')	WP	R9
Horta (rue Baron)	B	J6
Hoste (rue Julius)	Sc	O1
Hôtel des Monnaies (r.)	SG	H9-10
Hottat (rue Alphonse)	XL	LM10
Houblon (rue du)	B	G5

STREETS	PARISH COUNCILS	PLAN
Houffalize (place de)	Sc	L2
Houille (quai à la)	B	H4
Houilleurs (rue des)	Mo	G4
Houtmeyers ((rue J.)	Ev	P1
Houwaert (place)	SJ	L4
Houyoux (rue du)	Au	P11
Houzeau de Lehaie(rue)	Ko-Mo	F3
Hugo (rue Victor)	Sc	O5
Huygens (rue)	Mo	C4
Hydraulique (rue)	SJ	KL6
Hymans (rue Paul)	Sc	P3-4

• I •

Idalle (rue d')	XL	K8
Impens (rue Josse)	Sc	MN3
Impératrice (bld. de l')	B	I6
Imprimerie (rue de l')	Fo	E10
Indépendance (r. de l')	Mo	E4
Industrie (quai de l')	An-Mo	D7-E6-F5
Industrie (rue de l')	B	K7
Infante Isabelle (r.de l')	B	I6
Infirmerie (impasse de l') (rue de Laeken 63)	B	HI4-5
Infirmerie (rue de l')	B	H4
Initiative (pl. de l')	BA	A1
Inquisition (rue de l')	B	M5
Institut (rue de l')	An	A8
Instruction (rue de l')	An-SG	EF8
Intendant (rue de l')	Mo	FG2-G3
Irlande (rue d')	SG	HI11
Ixelles (chaus. d')	XL	J8-9-K9-10
Ixelles (galerie d')	XL	J8

• J •

Jacinthes (av. des)	Sc	N2
Jacobs (av. Victor)	Et	M10
Jacobs (place Jean)	B	I9
Jacobs (rue Pierre-Vic.)	Mo	G2
Jacqmain (bld. Emile)	B	I4

STREETS	PARISH COUNCILS	PLAN
Jacques (bld. Gn.)	Et-XL	M12-N12-O11
Jacquet (rue Jean)	Ko	E3
Jacquet (sq. Léon)	XL	I12
Jamar (bld.)	SG	FG8
Jansen (rue Jacques)	Sc	N4
Janson (pl. Paul)	SG	I11
Janson (r. Paul-Emile)	B-XL	J10
Janssen (rue J.B.)	Mo	D4
Janssen (rue)	An	B8
Janvier (av. de)	WL	R5
Jardin aux Fleurs (place du)	B	G5-6
Jardin Botanique	SJ	JK4
Jardin Botanique (bld. du)	B	J4
Jardin des Olives (rue)	B	H6
Jardinier (rue du)	Mo	F3
Jardin Rompu (rue du)	B	H7
Jardins (av. des)	Sc	P2-3
Jaspar (av. Henri)	SG	H9
Jean de Paduwa (pl)	Ev	R3
Jenatzy (rue)	Sc	L2
Jennart (rue)	Mo	FG3
Jenner (rue)	XL	LM8
Jérusalem (rue de)	Sc	M1-2
Jette (av. de)	JP-Ko	E1
Jette (ch. de)	JP-Ko	E1-F2-3
Jeu de Balle (pl. du)	B	H8
Jeunesse (av. de la)	Sc	P3
Jeunesse (rue de la)	Mo	D2-E3
Jolly (rue)	Sc	J1
Joly (sq. Dr. Jean)	Et	N10
Jonas (rue A.)	An	B6
Jonchaie (rue de la)	Et	O8
Jonction (av. de la)	Fo-SG	H12
Jonnart (av. Albert)	WL	P7
Jonniaux (rue)	Et	N8
Jordaens (rue J.)	B	K12
Jordens (sq. Charles)	SG	F10
Jorez (rue)	An	E7
Josaphat (rue)	SJ-Sc	L1-2-3
Joseph II (rue)	BK	LM6
Joséphine-Charlotte (square)	WL	R7-8
Joset (av. Camille)	Et	O9
Jottrand (avenue)	SJ	L4-5
Joubert (rue Capt.)	Et	P10-11
Jourdan (place)	Et	M8
Jourdan (rue)	SG	HI9
Joyeuse Entrée (avenue de la)	B	N7
Jubilé (bld. du)	Mo	F2-G1
Juillet (av. de)	WL	R6
Jupiter (avenue)	Fo	FG12
Juste-Lipse (rue)	B	M7
Justice (place de la)	B	I7
Justice (rue de la)	An	BC8

● K ●

STREETS	PARISH COUNCILS	PLAN
Karreveld (avenue du)	Ko-Mo	C3
Kelchtermans (rue J.)	An	A6
Keller (rue Ad.)	Au	P12
Kennedy (av. J.F.)	B	N7
Kennis (rue Guillaume)	Sc	N1
Kerckx (rue)	XL	L10
Kessels (rue)	Sc	L2
Keyenveld (rue)	XL	J9
Kindermans (rue)	B-XL	K11
Kinet (rue)	An	B8
Kips (rue Richard)	Et	N9
Klauwaerts (av. des)	XL	L12
Knapen (rue)	Sc	Q5-6
Koekelberg (av. de)	BA	A2
Korenberg (rue du)	Mo	AB3
De Koninck (rue)	Mo	BC3-4
Kouter (av. du)	Au	R12
Krains (rue Hubert)	Sc	O1-2
Krings (rue Albert)	Au	R12
Kuborn (rue Dr.)	An	DE9
Kuhnen (rue Willem)	Sc	N1
Kurth (rue Godefroid)	Ev	OP1

● L ●

STREETS	PARISH COUNCILS	PLAN
Labarre (rue Ant.)	XL	L11

STREETS	PARISH COUNCILS	PLAN
Lac (rue du)	B-XL	K11
Lacaille (rue)	B	G8
La Chasse	Et	N10
Lacomblé (av. Ad.)	Sc	P5
Lacomblé (rue Rd.)	Et	Q9
Laeken (rue de)	B	HI4-5
Laekenveld (rue)	Mo	G1
Laermans (rue Eug.)	Mo	G3
Lainé (sq.)	Fo	F12
Laines (rue aux)	B	I8
Laiterie (rue de la)	An	B5
Lalaing (rue J. de)	B	L7
Lambeau (av.)	WL	QR6
Lambeaux (av. Jef)	SG	H11
Lambermont (bld.)	Sc	N1-2
Lambermont (rue)	B	K7
Lambert (rue Baron)	Et	N9
Lambiotte (rue Aug.)	Sc	N4
Lance (av. de la)	Ev	Q3
Lanfray (rue)	XL	L11
Lannoy (rue)	XL	K11
Lartigue (rue Gén.)	WL	Q6
Larousse (square)	Fo	H12
Latinis (av. Gustave)	Sc	N1-2
Laude (rue Ernest)	Sc	LM1
Laure (av.)	BA	A2
Lausanne (rue de)	SG	I10
Lavallée (rue Adolphe)	Mo	G3
Lavigerie (r. Cardinal)	Et	P10-11
Lavoir (rue du)	B	G8
Lebeau (rue)	B	I7
Lebon (av. G.-E.)	Au-WP	Q11-12
Lebrun (rue J.)	Sc	P4
Lecharlier (av. Firmin)	JP	F1
Lechat (rue Charles)	Au	R12
Leclercq (rue G.-J.)	Au	Q12
Le Corrège (rue)	B	N6
Leduc (rue Paul)	Sc	P3
Leemans (pl. Albert)	XL	J12
Lefever (avenue G.)	Au	Q12
Lefèvre (rue Victor)	Sc	O6
Lefrancq (rue)	Sc	K2
Legrain (av. des Frères)	WP	Q10
Legrelle (rue Charles)	Et	PQ9
Lehon (place)	Sc	KL2

STREETS	PARISH COUNCILS	PLAN
Le Lorrain (rue)	Mo	GH2
Leman (rue Général)	Et	MN8
Le Marinet (avenue)	Et	P10
Lemmens (place A.)	An	F6
Lemonnier (bld. Maurice)	B	GH6-7
Lemonnier (rue C.)	XL	J12
Lenglentier (rue de)	B	G8
Lens (rue)	B-XL	K10-11
Léopold (rue)	B	I5
Léopold II (bld.)	Ko-Mo	F2-G3
Léopold II (square)	WP	R8-9
Léopold III (av.)	Ev	P1-2-3
Léopold III (bld.)	Sc	P2-3
Léopoldville (sq. de)	Et	M10
Lepage (rue Léon)	B	GH5
Lepoutre (av. Louis)	XL	IJ12
Lepreux (rue Omer)	Ko	C1
Leroy (pl. Edmond)	Mo	B3
Lesbroussart (rue)	B-XL	K10
Lessines (rue de)	Mo	DE5
Le Tintoret (rue)	B	N6
Le Titien (rue)	B	N6
Levallois-Perret (r. de)	Mo	AB5
Levant (rue du)	XL	L12
Levie (sq.)	Sc	Q6
Levure (rue de la)	XL	L10
Leys (rue)	B	O7
Libérateurs (sq. des)	Mo	F2
Liberté (avenue de la)	Ko-Mo	CDE2
Liberté (place de la)	B	K5
Libre Examen (rue du)	An	C8
Licorne (av. de la)	WL	R5
Licorne (clos de la)	WL	R5
Liedekerke (rue de)	SJ	L5
Liedts (place)	Sc	K2
Liedts (rue)	Sc	K2
Liégeois (rue des)	XL	LM10
Lierre (rue du)	Mo	D4
Liétard (rue Maurice)	WP	Q9
Lilas (rue du)	B	H4
Limauge (rue)	XL	L9
Limite (rue de la)	SJ	KL4
Limnander (rue)	An	F7
Linière (rue de la)	SG	H9

STREETS	PARISH COUNCILS	PLAN
Linné (rue)	Sc-SJ	J3
Linthout (rue de)	Et-Sc-WL	O6-P6-7
Lippens (rue Lieut.)	Et	O10
Lisbonne (rue de)	SG	G10
Liverpool (rue de)	An-Mo	F6
Livingstone (av.)	B	L6
Livourne (rue de)	B-SG-XL	J10-11
Locquenghien (rue)	B	GH4
Loi (rue de la)	B	JK6
Loix (place)	SG	I9
Lombard (rue du)	B	HI6
Lombardie (rue de)	SG	H11
Loncin (rue de)	SG	G11
Londres (place de)	XL	K8
Londres (rue de)	XL	K8
Longtin (rue)	JP	F1
Longueville (av. Gn.)	WP	R9-10
Longue Haie (r. de la)	B-XL	J9-10
Longue Vie (rue de)	XL	K8-9
Lorand (rue Georges)	XL	K9
Loriot (av. du)	WP	R12
Lothaire (av. Cdt)	Et	PQ10
Louise (avenue)	B-SG-XL	I9-J10-K9-10
Louise (galerie)	XL	IJ9
Louise (place)	B	I8-9
Louvain (chaussée de)	Ev	QR3
Louvain (chaussée de)	SJ-Sc	KLM N5-OP4
Louvain (place de)	B	J6
Louvain (porte de)	B	K5
Louvain (rue de)	B	K6
Loxum (rue de)	B	IJ6
Luther (rue)	B	MN5
Luxembourg (pl. du)	XL	L8
Luxembourg (rue du)	B-XL	K7-8
Luzerne (rue de la)	Sc	O4
Lycée (rue du)	SG	H10-11
Lynen (rue Amdée)	SJ	L5
Lys (rue de la)	Mo	F1-2

STREETS	PARISH COUNCILS	PLAN
● M ●		
Ma Campagne	SG	I11
Macau (av. Guil.)	XL	L11
Machtens (sq. Edm.)	Mo	B5
Machtens (bld. Edm.)	Mo	ABC5-D4
Madeleine (rue de la)	B	I6
Madou (place)	B	K5
Madoux (av. Charles)	Au	P11
Maelbeek (av. du)	B-Et	M8
Maes (rue)	XL	KL10
Magasin (rue du)	B	H4
Magistrat (rue du)	B-XL	JK11
Mahatma Gandhi (av.)	Ko	E3
Mahillon (av. Léon)	Sc	O5
Mai (av. de)	WL	QR6
Mai (pl. de)	WL	R6
Mail de la Haquenée	Ev	Q3
Mail (rue du)	XL	J11-12
Malherbe (rue Fr.)	An	C7-8
Malibran (pet. rue)	XL	L10
Malibran (rue)	XL	L9-10
Malines (rue de)	B	I4
Malis (rue Ch.)	Mo	BC4
Malou (av. Jules)	Et	N9-10
Manchester (rue de)	Mo	E5-6
Manne (rue)	An	A7
Maquis (rue du)	Ev	R2-3
Marais (rue du)	B	J4-5
Marbotin (rue Ad.)	Sc	NO1
Marcette (rue Alex)	Et	N10
Marchal (av. Félix)	Sc	NO5
Marché-au-Bois	B	J6
Marché-au-Charbon (r.)	B	H6
Marché-au-Fromages	B	I6
Marché-aux-Herbes (rue du)	B	I6
Marché-aux-Peaux	B	I6
Marché-aux-Porcs	B	H4
Marché-aux-Poulets (rue du)	B	H5
Marconi (rue)	Fo	G12
Marcq (rue)	B	H4
Marcx (rue L.)	Au	Q11-12

STREETS	PARISH COUNCILS	PLAN
Marguerite (square)	B	N6
Marichal (rue Henri)	XL	M11
Marie de Bourgogne(r.)	B-XL	KL7
Marie-Henriette (avenue Reine)	Fo	F12
Marie-Henriette (rue)	XL	L10
Marie-José (av.)	WL	QR6
Marie-José (sq.)	WL	R6
Marie-Louise (square)	B	LM6
Mariemont (quai de)	Mo	E6
Marie-Thérèse (rue)	B-SJ	L5-6
Mariniers (rue des)	Mo	G4
Markelbach (rue Alex.)	Sc	MN4
Marne (rue de la)	Sc	K2
Marnix (avenue)	B	J8
Maroquain (rue du)	Mo	G4
Marquis (rue du)	B	H6
Marronnier (rue du)	B	H4-5
Mars (av. de)	WL	Q5-6
Marteau (rue du)	B-SJ	L6
Martel (rue Charles)	B	M6
Martin (rue J.G.)	WL-WP	R8
Martyrs (place des)	B	I5
Mascré (rue L.)	An	C7
Massart (rue Jean)	Et	OP9
Massaux (rue)	Sc	L3-4
Massenet (avenue)	Fo	EF12
Masui (rue)	B2-Sc	IJ1
Matériaux (quai des)	B2	H2-3
Matériaux (rue des)	An	D7
Matheus (rue Georges)	SJ	IJ3
Mathieu (rue Ad.)	XL	M11
Maus (rue Henri)	B	H6
Max (av. Emile)	Sc	OP5
Max (bld. Adolphe)	B	I4
Mégissiers (rue des)	An	F6
Meiboom (rue du)	B	J5
Meiser (pl. Gén.)	Sc	OP4
Mélèzes (rue des)	XL	J12
Mélodie (rue de la)	Mo	D4
Melon (rue du)	Fo	E12
Mélopée (rue de la)	Mo	C4-5
Melpomène (rue)	Mo	C4
Melsens (rue)	B	H5
Memling (rue)	An	F7
Ménages (rue des)	B	G8-9
Ménapiens (rue des)	Et	P7-8
Ménestrels (av. des)	An-Mo	AB5
Menin (rue de)	Mo	E4
Mennekens (pl. Jef)	Mo	C4
Menuisier (rue du)	WL	R7
Mercelis (rue)	B-XL	J9-10
Merchtem (ch. de)	Mo	F3-4
Mercier (rue Card.)	B	I6
Merckaert (rue Jules)	Sc	P3
Méridien (rue du)	SJ	K4
Mérinos (rue du)	SJ	L4
Merjay (rue Frans)	XL	I12
Mérode (rue de)	Fo-SG	E10-F9-G8
Mesens (avenue Ed.)	Et	Q10
Métairie (rue de la)	BA	BC1
Métal (rue du)	SG	H10
Métaux (rue des)	Et	M8-9
Metsys (rue)	Sc	L1
Mettewie (bld. L.)	Mo-Ko	AB4-BC3
Meurice (rue Albert)	Et	N8
Meuse (rue de la)	Mo	F1-2
Mexico (rue de)	Mo	G3
Michel-Ange (av.)	B	N6
Midi (bld. du)	B	G7
Midi (rue du)	B	H6-7
Miesse (square Jules et Edm.)	An	DE8
Mignon (rue Léon)	Sc	N4-5
Milcamps (av. Achille)	Sc	O4-5
Mimosas (av. des)	WP	Q10-11
Mimosas (rue des)	Sc	N2
Minimes (pet. rue des)	B	I7
Minimes (rue des)	B	HI7-8
Miroir (rue du)	B	H7-8
Missionnaires (av. d.)	An-Mo	B5-6
Moerkerke (rue de)	Sc	K1
Moineaux (rue des)	B	H6
Moines (rue des)	Fo	E10
Moissonneurs (rue des)	Et	O9-10
Moissons (rue des)	SJ	L4
Molignée (rue de la)	Au	P11
Molitor (rue Général)	Et	O10

STREETS	PARISH COUNCILS	PLAN
Mommaerts (rue)	Mo	G3
Mommaerts (av. L.)	Sc-Ev	QR4
Monastère (rue du)	B-XL	L12
Moniteur (rue du)	B	J5
Monnaie (pl. de la)	B	I5
Monnet (carrefour Jean)	B	M6
Monrose (rue)	Sc	M3-4
Mons (chaus. de)	An	CD8-EF7
Montagne (rue de la)	B	I6
Montagne aux Anges (rue)	Ko	F3
Montagne de la Cour	B	J7
Montagne-aux-Herbes-Potagères (rue)	B	I5
Montagne-de-l'Oratoire (r.)	B	J5
Montagne du Parc (rue)	B	J6
Mont-Blanc (rue du)	S	GH10
Mont des Arts	B	I6-7
Mont du Chêne (rue)	Et	N10
Mont du Cinquantenaire	Et	O8
Monténégro (rue du)	Fo-SG	E11-F10-11
Montgomery (square)	WP	Q8
Mont-Kemmel (av. du)	Fo-SG	G11-12
Montoyer (rue)	B-XL	KL7
Montserrat (rue)	B	H8-9
Moranville (rue de)	JP	EF1
Moreau (rue Georges)	An	E8
Moretus (rue)	An	F7
Morichar (pl. Louis)	SG	H10
Morins (rue des)	Et	PQ8
Moris (rue)	SG	HI11
Morjau (rue Jean)	An	A8
Moscou (rue de)	SG	H9-10
Mosselmans (rue J.B.)	Ev	OP1
Moucherons (rue des)	B	H6
Mouettes (av.des)	WP	R11
Moulin (rue du)	SJ	L4
Murillo (rue)	B	O6-7
Mus (rue Fr.)	Mo	G1
Musée (petite rue du)	B	IJ7
Musée (place du)	B	I7
Muse (rue du)	B	J7
Musin (rue)	SJ	K4
Myrtes (av. des)	Mo	A3

● N ●

STREETS	PARISH COUNCILS	PLAN
Namur (porte de)	B	J8
Namur (rue de)	B	J7-8
Nancy (rue de)	B	H8
Naples (rue de)	XL	K8
Natation (rue de la)	XL	LM9
Nation (place de la)	B	JK6
Nations (galerie des)	SJ	I4
Navets (rue des)	B	G6
Neep (rue du)	B2	E3
Nicolay (rue)	B2	I3
Nid (rue du)	XL	L11
Nerviens (av. des)	B-Et	NO8
Neuchâtel (rue de)	SG	I10
Neuray (rue Fern.)	XL	I12
Neuve (rue)	B	I4-5
Neuvième de Ligne (boulevard du)	B	GH3-4
Newton (rue)	B	NO6
Nieuport (bd. de)	B	G4
Nieuwmolen (rue du)	An	E9
Ninove (chaussée de)	An-Mo	AB6-CDEF5
Ninove (place et porte de)	B	FG5
Niveau (rue du)	Mo	F4
Nivelles (dr. de)	Au-WP	QR10-11
Nogent (rue Henri)	Mo	BC3
Nom de Jésus (rue du)	B	H5
Nord (passage du)	B	I5
Nord (petite rue du)	B	K5
Nord (place du)	SJ	J3
Nord (rue du)	B	K5
Normandie (rue de)	Ko	DE2
Norvège (rue de)	SG	F9
Nothomb (rue)	Et	N10
Notre-Dame-de-Fatima (avenue)	BA	B1
Notre-Dame-des-Grâces (rue)	B	H8
Notre-Dame-du-Sommeil (rue)	B	G5
Notre-Seigneur (rue)	B	H7
Nouveau Marché-aux-		

STREETS	PARISH COUNCILS	PLAN
Grains (place du)	B	G5
Nouvelle (avenue)	Et	M10-N11
Noville (sq.)	Ko	F3
Noyer (rue du)	B-Sc	N5-O6

● O ●

STREETS	PARISH COUNCILS	PLAN
Obus (rue de l')	An	B7
Octobre (rue d')	WL	R5
Odon (rue)	An	F6
Œillets (rue des)	B	I5
Oiseau Bleu (av. de l')	WP	QR10
Olivier (pet. rue de l')	Sc	L3
Olivier (rue de l')	Sc	KL3
Ombrages (av. des)	WL	R8
Ommegang (rue de l')	B	J5
Ongena (rue)	JP	F1
Onze Novembre (av.du)	Et	O9
Opale (av. de l')	Sc	O6-P5
Openveld (rue)	BA	A1
Ophem (rue d')	B	H4
Optimisme (av. de l')	Ev	Q3
Orban (rue Alfred)	Fo	E10-11
Orchidées (rue des)	An	C8
Orfèvres (r. des) (Cité)	B	H8
Orient (rue de l')	Et	M9
Orion (av.)	WL	R5
Orme (rue de l')	Et-Sc	P6-O7
Orphelinat (rue de l')	An	B6-7
Ortélius (rue)	B	L6
Orts (rue Auguste)	B	H5
Osiers (rue des)	Mo	F4
Osseghem (rue)	Mo	B5-CD4
Ostendael (rue)	Mo	C4
Ostende (rue d')	Mo	EF4
Otlet (rue)	An	F7
Oudart (rue V.)	Sc	O5
Ouest (place de l')	Mo	E4
Ours (rue de l')	AN	A6
Ourthe (rue de l')	Mo	F2

● P ●

STREETS	PARISH COUNCILS	PLAN
Pachéco (bld.)	B	J4-5
Pacification (rue de la)	B-SJ	L5-6
Padoue (rue de)	Fo	E10
Paepedelle (av. du)	Au	Q11-12
Page (rue du)	XL	IJ11-I12
Paille (rue de la)	B	I7
Paix (av. de la)	Ko	C1-2
Paix (rue de la)	XL	JK8
Palais (place des)	B	J7
Palais (rue des)	Sc	K1-2-3
Palmerston (avenue)	B	M6
Palmiers (rue des)	WP	Q10-11
Pangaert (rue)	Ga	C1
Panthéon (av. du)	Ko	C1-D2-E3
Pâquerettes (rue des)	Sc	M2-3
Paquot (rue Jean)	XL	L10-M11
Parade (allée de la)	Ev	Q3
Paradis (rue du)	B	I7
Paradisiers (av. des)	Au-WP	R11-12
Parc (avenue du)	Fo-SG	FG11
Parc Elisabeth (rue du)	Ko	E2
Parc Josaphat	Sc	M1-2-N3
Parenthé (rue Charles)	An	E9
Parfums (rue des)	An	B7-8
Paris (rue de)	B-XL	K8
Parlement (galerie du)	B	K5
Parlement (rue du)	B	JK6
Parme (rue de)	SG	H10
Parnasse (rue du)	XL	KL8
Paroissiens (rue des)	B	J6
Paruck (rue du)	Mo	D3
Passage 44	B	J4
Passchendaele (rue de)	B	GH4
Passereaux (av. des)	Au-WP	R12
Pasteur (rue)	An	E8
Pastorale (rue de la)	An-Mo	A5
Patrie (place de la)	Sc	NO4
Patriotes (rue des)	B	NO6
Paulsen (bld. Félix)	An	A7
Pavez (rue J.)	An	B8
Pavie (rue de)	B	M5-6
Pavillon (place du)	Sc	KL1
Pavillon (rue du)	Sc	K1

STREETS	PARISH COUNCILS	PLAN
Pavots (rue des)	Sc	O4
Pavoux (rue Eug.)	Mo	E5
Paysagistes (rue des)	Au	Q12
Pays de Liège (rue)	B	H4
Pégasse (av.)	WL	R5
Pélican (rue du)	B	I4
Pelletier (rue Fréd.)	Sc	P6
Pène (rue du)	B	G5
Péniches (quai des)	B2	H2-3
Pennion (av. du)	Ev	Q3
Pensées (rue des)	Sc	N2
Pepin (rue du)	B	J8
Pépinière (rue de la)	B	J7-8
Pequeur (sq. Rob)	An	F7
Perche (rue de la)	SG	G10
Perdrix (rue des)	Et	O9-10
Pères Blancs (rue des)	Et	P11
Père Pire (rue)	Mo	D3
Perle (rue de la)	Mo	F4
Persil (rue du)	B	I5
Pervyse (rue de)	Et	P9-10
Petillon (rue Major)	Et	P10
Petit (rue Gabrielle)	Mo	G1
Petit Berchem (rue du)	BA	B1-2
Petit Rempart (rue du)	B	G6
Petits-Carmes (r. des)	B	IJ8
Pêtre (av. Georges)	SJ	LM5
Peuple (rue du)	B2	I3
Peuplier (rue du)	B	H5
Pfeiffer (rue Martin)	Mo	C3
Philantropie (rue de la)	B	G9
Pilippe-de-Champagne (rue)	B	H7
Philippe-le-Bon (rue)	B	L6
Philomène (rue)	Sc	L4
Picard (rue)	Mo	GH2
Pieremans (rue)	B	H8-9
Piermez (rue Phil.)	Ko	E3
Pierres (rue des)	B	H6
Pierres de Taille (quai aux)	B	H4
Pierron (rue Evariste)	Mo	F5
Piers (rue)	Mo	FG3
Piétons (rue des)	SJ	J3
Pigeons (rue des)	B	I7
Pinsons (av. des)	WP	R11-12
Pirmez (rue Eudore)	Et	N10
Piron (av. Brigade)	Mo	C3-4
Plaine (bld. de la)	XL	O12
Plaine des Manœuvres	XL	OP12
Plantes (rue des)	SC-SJ	J3
Plantin (rue)	An	F7
Plasky (av. Eugène)	Sc	O4-5
Plasky (sq. Eugène)	Sc	O5
Platanes (rue des)	Et	N9
Plateau (rue Joseph)	B	H5
Plattesteen (rue)	B	H6
Plétinckx (rue)	B	GH6
Plisnier (av. Charles)	An	A7-8
Plissart (rue Nestor)	Et-WP	Q9
Plume (rue de la)	B	G8
Poelaert (place)	B	I8
Pogge (place)	Sc	L1
Poincaré (bld. R.)	B	G6-7
Poinçon (rue du)	B	H7
Poissonniers (rue des)	B	H5
Poivre (rue du)	B	I6
Pôle (rue du)	SJ	K4
Pologne (rue de)	SG	H11
Pont de la Carpe (rue)	B	H5
Ponthier (rue Com.)	Et	OP10
Pont-Levis (rue du)	WL	R7
Pont-Neuf (rue du)	B	I4
Porselein (rue)	An	A8
Port (avenue du)	B2-Mo	H1-2-3-I1
Porte de Hal (av. de la)	SG	G8-9
Porte Rouge (rue de la)	B	H8
Portugal (rue du)	SG	H11
Posschier (rue)	Et	M8-9
Poste (rue de la)	Sc-SJ	K2-3
Postes (passage des)	B	H5
Potaerdegat (rue)	Mo	B3
Potaerdenberg (rue du)	An-Mo	A7-8
Potagère (rue)	Sc-SJ	K5-L4
Poterie (pet. rue de la)	An	F6
Poterie (rue de la)	An	F6
Potiers (rue des)	B	G6
Poudrière (rue de la)	B	G5
Prado (rue du)	Mo	F4

STREETS	PARISH COUNCILS	PLAN
Prague (rue de)	SG	G10
Prairie (rue de la)	SJ	J3
Préau (avenue du)	Et	N9
Prekelinden (avenue)	WL	Q6-7
Presbytère (rue du)	Mo	F3
Président (rue du)	XL	J9
Presse (rue de la)	B	K5-6
Prétoire (rue du)	An	B8
Prêtres (rue des)	B	H9
Prévinaire (rue)	An	D8
Prévost Delaunay (sq.)	Sc	NO3
Prévôt (rue du)	XL	I-J12
Prévoyance (rue de la)	B	H9
Prince de Liège(bld. du)	An	A6-7
Prince Héritier (av. du)	WL	QR6-7
Prince Royal (rue du)	XL	J9
Princes (galeries des)	B	I6
Princes (rue des)	B	I5
Princesse (rue de la)	Mo	E5
Printemps (rue du)	XL	N12
Procession (rue de la)	AN	A8
Progrès (rue du)	Sc-SJ	J3-4
Prospérité (rue de la)	Mo	G4
Puccini (rue)	An	AB6
Putterie	B	I6

● Q ●

STREETS	PARISH COUNCILS	PLAN
Quatre-Août (pl. du)	Et	P9
Quatre-Bras (rue des)	B	I8
Quatrecht (rue de)	Sc	JK3
Quatre Fils Aymon (rue des)	B	I7
Quatre Journées de Septembre (bld. des)	SJ	M5
Quatre Vents (rue des)	Mo	E4-5-F4
Querelle (rue de la)	B	G8
Quetelet (place)	SJ	K5
Quiétude (av. de la)	Ev	QR3
Quiétude (sq. de la)	WP	R10
Quinaux (rue)	Sc	L1

● R ●

STREETS	PARISH COUNCILS	PLAN
Radis (rue des)	B	GH8
Radium (rue du)	Sc	NO5
Rameurs (rue des)	B2	IJ1
Ramoneurs (rue des) (Cité)	B	H8-9
Ramskapelle (rue de)	Et	P10
Ransfort (rue)	Mo	F5
Raphaël (rue)	An	E7
Rasière (rue de la)	B	H8
Raskin (rue M.A.)	An	A7
Rasson (rue)	Sc	O5-6
Ravenstein (galerie)	B	J6
Ravenstein (rue)	B	J6
Rayé (rue Jacques)	Sc	M1
Raymond (rue J.E.)	Au	Q11
Rectangle (rue du)	Mo	F5
Réforme (rue de la)	XL	I12
Régates (rue des)	B2	J1
Régence (rue de la)	B	IJ7
Régent (bld. du)	B	K6
Reigersvliet (rue de)	Et	N11
Reine (av. de la)	Sc	JK1-2
Reine (gal. de la)	B	I6
Reine (place de la)	Sc	K3
Reine (rue de la)	B	I5
Reinette (rue de la)	B	J8
Relais Sacré (rue du)	Ko	F3
Remblai (rue du)	B	G9
Rembrandt (rue)	B	N6
Rempart des Moines (rue)	B	G5
Remy (rue Georges)	BA	B1
Renaissance (av. de la)	B	NO7
Renan (av. Ernest)	Sc	M1
Renards (rue des)	B	H8
Rency (rue G.)	WL	Q6
Renkin (rue)	Sc	K1-2
Repos (place du)	An	B7
Requette (av. Carl)	Mo	AB4
Résidence (sq. de la)	XL	KL8
Résistance (pl. de la)	An	BC8
Révision (bld. de la)	An	E8-9
Révolution (rue de la)	B	K5
Rey (sq. Henri)	An	AB6-7
Reyers (bld. Auguste)	Sc	P4-5-6
Rhétorique (rue de la)	SG	H10

STREETS	PARISH COUNCILS	PLAN
Ribaucourt (rue de)	Mo	G2-3
Riches-Claires (rue des)	B	H6
Richir (rue H.)	Sc	O1
Riethuisen (av. Vital)	Ga	D1
Rinsdelle (place du)	Et	O9
Rivière (rue de la)	SJ	J3-4
Rivoli (rue)	B	J5
Robiano (rue de)	Sc	L3
Robie (rue Jean)	SG	G11
Rochefort (place de)	Fo	F11
Rodenbach (rue)	Fo	G12
Rodin (av. Auguste)	XL	M10-11
Roelandts (rue)	SC	L3
Roffiaen (rue Fr.)	XL	M12
Rogations (av. des)	WL	PQ7
Rogier (avenue)	SC	LMN3-O4
Rogier (place)	SJ	J4
Rogier (rue)	B2-SG	J2
Roi (avenue du)	Fo-SG	F10-11
Roi (galerie du)	B	I6
Roi Vainqueur (pl. du)	Et	OP9
Roland (rue Arthur)	Sc	O2
Rollebeek (rue de)	B	I7
Rome (rue de)	SG	GH10
Rond-Point (av. Louise)	B	K12
Roodebeek (av. de)	Sc	OPQ5
Roodebeek (chauss. de)	WL	QR5
Roosevelt (rue Th.)	Sc	O6
Ropsy-Chaudron (rue)	An	E6-7
Rosacées (clos des)	Mo	A4
Rosée (rue de la)	An	F6
Roses (rue des)	B	I5
Rossini (rue)	An	EF8
Rostand (rue Ed.)	An	B6
Rotterdam (rue de)	Mo	G1
Roue (rue de la)	Mo	G1
Roue (rue de la)	B	H7
Rouen-Bovie (rue)	SJ	M4-5
Rouleau (rue du)	B	H4-5
Roumanie (rue de)	SG	H10
Rouppe (place)	B	H7
Rouppe (rue)	B	H7
Royale (place)	B	J7
Royale (rue)	B-Sc-SJ	K3-4
Royale-Ste-Marie (rue)	Sc	K2-3-L1

STREETS	PARISH COUNCILS	PLAN
Ruanda (rue du)	Et	O9
Rubens (rue)	Sc	KL1
Ruche (rue de la)	Sc	L2
Rucquoy (rue Gén.)	An	C6
Ruhl (rue Jules)	An	E6
Ruisselet (clos du)	BA	A1
Rudder (rue)	Mo	CD3
Ruisseau (rue du)	Mo	G3-4
Russie (rue de)	SG	G8
Ruysbroek (rue de)	B	I7
Ruysdael (rue)	An	E7
Ryckmans (r. Hélène)	Mo	3-4

● S ●

STREETS	PARISH COUNCILS	PLAN
Sables (rue des)	B	J5
Sablon (pl. du Grand)	B	I7
Sablon (pl. du Petit)	B	I8
Sablonnière (rue de la)	B	K5
Sablons (rue des)	B	I7
Sagittaire (av. du)	WL	R5
Sainctelette (place)	Mo	H3
Sainctelette (square)	B	H3
Saulnier (rue A. de)	Mo	B3
St.-Alphonse (rue)	SJ	KL5
St.-André (rue)	B	H4
St.-Antoine (parvis)	Fo	E10
St.-Antoine (place)	Et	N10
St.-Bernard (rue)	SG	I10
St.-Boniface (rue)	XL	J8
St.-Christophe (rue)	B	H6
St.-Esprit (rue du)	B	H7
St.-François (rue)	SJ	JK4
St.-Géry (place)	B	H6
St.-Géry (rue)	B	H6
St.-Georges (rue)	XL	K12
St.-Ghislain (rue)	B	H8
St.-Gilles (parvis)	SG	G10
St.-Guidon (rue)	An	A8
St.-Henri (parvis)	WL	Q7
St.-Henri (rue)	WL	Q7
St.-Honoré (passage)	B	HI5
St.-Hubert (gal.)	B	I6
St.-Hubert (rue)	WP	QR9
St.-Jean (place)	B	I6
St.-Jean (rue)	B	I6

STREETS	PARISH COUNCILS	PLAN
St.-Jean-Baptiste (par.)	Mo	G4
St.-Jean-Népomucène (rue)	B	I4
St.-Joseph (rue)	Ev	R3
St.-Joseph (rue)	Mo	F3-4
St.-Josse (place)	SJ	L5
St.-Josse (rue)	SJ	L5
St.-Julien (rue)	M	oF3
St.-Laurent (rue)	B	J5
St.-Lazare (bld.)	SJ	J4
St.-Lazare (place)	SJ	J3
St.-Lazare (rue)	SJ	J4
St.-Martin (rue)	Mo	F5
St.-Michel (bld.)	Et-WP	Q8-9
St.-Michel (rue)	B	I5
St.-Pierre (chaussée)	Et	MNO8
St.-Pierre (place)	Et	O8
St.-Pierre (rue)	B	I4
St.-Quentin (rue)	B	M6
St.-Roch (rue)	B	I4
Ste.-Adresse (pl. de)	An	A8
Ste.-Anne (rue)	B	I7
Ste.-Catherine (place)	B	H5
Ste.-Catherine (rue)	B	H5
Ste.-Croix (place)	XL	L11
Ste.-Gertrude (rue)	Et	N8
Ste.-Gudule (place)	B	J6
Ste.-Gudule (rue)	B	I6
Ste.-Marie (rue)	Mo	G4
Ste.-Thérèse (rue)	B	G8
Saisons (av. des)	XL	N12
Sallaert (rue)	B	G8
Samaritaine (rue de la)	B	I7
Sambre (rue de la)	Mo	G1
Samedi (place du)	B	H5
Sans-Souci (rue)	XL	KL9
Sans-Souci (square)	XL	L9
Saphir (rue du)	Sc	OP4
Savoie (rue de)	SG	GH11
Savonnerie (rue de la)	Mo	EF4-5
Saxe-Cobourg (rue de)	SJ	KL5
Scailquin (rue)	SJ	KL5
Scampart (rue Léon)	Et	O9
Scarron (rue)	XL	KL10
Sceptre (rue du)	XL	LM9
Schaerbeek (porte de)	B	K4

STREETS	PARISH COUNCILS	PLAN
Schaerbeek (rue de)	B	JK4-5
Schettler (avenue A.)	WP	R11
Scheut (avenue de)	An	BC7
Scheutbosch (av. du)	Mo	A5
Scheutveld (rue)	An	C8
Schmidt (bld. Louis)	Et	P10
Schmitz (rue)	Ko	EF3
Schols (rue Joseph)	Mo	D3
Schoofs (av. Henri)	Au	OP11
Schuman (rond p. R.)	B	M7
Science (rue de la)	B	KL7
Sébastopol (rue de)	An	C8
Secours (pet. rue des)	Sc-SJ	K3
Secours (rue des)	S	JK3
Sécurité (rue de la)	Ko	F3
Segers (rue P.)	Et	M10
Seghers (avenue)	Ko-Mo	D2-3
Sel (rue du)	An	D8
Semence (rue de la)	Mo	C5
Senne (rue de la)	BG	6
Septembre (av.de)	WL	R6
Serbie (rue de)	Fo-SG	EF10
Sergijsels (rue Em.)	Ko	F3
Serkeyn (rue J.B.)	JP	F1-2
Serment (rue du)	An	AB8
Sermon (avenue J.)	Ga	D1
Serpentin (rue du)	XL	L10
Serpolet (rue du)	Mo	AB5
Serrure (rue de la)	B	G5
Servais-Kinet (rue A. et ML.)	WL	R6
Seutin (rue)	Sc	KL3
Sicambres (rue des)	Et	P9
Simoens (rue Camille)	Sc	L1
Simonis (pl. Eugène)	Ko	F2
Simonis (rue)	SG-X	LIJ11
Simons (rue)	B2	I3
Sincérité (rue de la)	An	B7
Six-Aunes (rue des)	B	I8
Six-Jetons (rue des)	BG	H6
Six-Jeunes-Hommes (rue des)	B	I7
Slegers (av. A.J.)	WL	R7
Smekens (rue A.)	Sc	Q5
Smets (av. Josse)	Au	Q12
Smets (square A.)	B-Mo	F5

STREETS	PARISH COUNCILS	PLAN
Smits (rue Jacob)	An	B7
Smits (rue Eugène)	Sc	M3
Sneessens (rue)	Et	N9
Socquet (rue Louis)	Sc	P4
Soignies (rue de)	B	G6
Soleil (rue du)	Sc-SJ	L4
Sols (rue des)	B	I6
Solvay (place)	Sc	J3
Solvay (rue Ernest)	XL	JK8
Sonnet (rue du)	Mo	C4
Source (rue de la)	SG	I9-10
Souvenir (rue du)	An	B7
Souvenir (square du)	XL	L11
Souverains (rue)	B-XL	JK9
Spa (rue de)	SG	F8
Spaak (rue Paul)	B-XL	K10
Speeckaert (av. Ed.)	WL	R6
Stade (rue de)	Fo	E12
Stacquet (rue Henri)	Sc	N3
Stalingrad (av. de)	B	G7
Stats (rue Jean)	SG	I9
Steamers (quai des)	B2	I1
Steens (rue L.)	SG	GH10
Stéphanie (place)	B-XL	I9
Stepman (rue)	Ko	E3
Sterckx (rue)	SG	G10
Steurs (pl. Arm.)	SJ	L4
Stevens (rue Joseph)	B	I7
Stévin (rue)	B	N7
Stijns (rue R.)	Mo	C3-4
Stobbaerts (av. Jean)	Sc	N3
Stocq (rue Guillaume)	XL	L11
Stratégie (rue de la)	Au	P11
Stroobant (rue Franá.)	XL	I12
Suède (rue de)	SG	FG9
Suffrage Universel (avenue du)	Sc	M1-2
Suisse (rue de)	SG	I9
Surlet de Chokier (pl.)	B	K5

● T ●

STREETS	PARISH COUNCILS	PLAN
Tabellion (rue du)	XL	I11
Tabora (rue de)	B	H6
Taciturne (rue du)	B	M6-7
Tamines (rue de)	SG	H11
Tanaris (av. des)	Mo	B4-5
Tannerie (rue de la)	Ko	E3
Tanneurs (rue des)	B	G8
Tasson Snel (rue)	SG	I10
Taziaux (rue)	Mo	F3
Teinturiers (rue des)	B	H6
Teirlinck (rue Isidore)	Mo	E5
Tell (rue Guillaume)	SG	G10
Temple (rue du)	B	H7
Tenbosch (rue)	B-XL	JK11
Teniers (rue)	Sc	LM2
Terarken (rue)	B	J7
Terlinden (rue Félix)	Et	N10
Terre-Neuve (rue)	B	H7
Tervaete (rue de)	Et	P9-10
Tervueren (av. de)	Et-WP	PQR8
Tervueren (porte de)	Et	O8
Tete d'Or (rue de la)	B	H6
Thérésienne (rue)	B	J7
Theux (rue de)	Et	M9-10
Thibault (av. Ed. de)	Et	O9
Thieffry (rue Aviateur)	Et	P9-10
Thiéfry (rue)	Sc	L3
Thiernesse (rue)	An	A7
Tiberghien (rue)	SJ	L4
Tilleul (rue du)	Sc	O1
Timmermans (rue)	Fo	FG12
Timmermans (rue J.B.)	WL	R6
Tir (rue du)	SG	F10
Tisserands (rue des)	Ko	E3
Titz (rue Louis)	Et	O8
't Kint (rue)	B	G6
Tocsin (rue du)	B	N6
Toison d'Or (av. de la)	XL-SG	I8-9
Toison d'Or (galerie)	XL-SG	J8
Tombeur (rue Gén.)	Et	O8-9
Tombu (avenue L.)	WL	R7
Tongres (rue des)	Et	P7-8
Tonneliers (rue des) (Cité)	B	H8
Topaze (av. de la)	Sc	O4-5
Topweg (rue)	JP	F1
Tornooiveld (av. du)	Ev	Q3
Toulouse (rue de)	B	L7
Tourelle (rue de la)	Et	M8

STREETS	PARISH COUNCILS	PLAN
Tournai (rue de)	B	G7
Tournesols (rue des)	An	A5-6
Tourterelles (av. des)	WP	R11
Toussaint (rue Fritz)	XL	MN11-12
Toxandres (rue des)	Et	P8
Transvaal (rue du)	An	D8
Traquets (av. des)	Au	R12
Travail (rue du)	B2	I1
Traversière (rue)	SJ	K4
Trèfle (clos du)	Au	R12
Treurenberg	B	J6
Trèves (rue de)	B-XL	L7
Trévires (rue des)	Et	P8
Triangle (place du)	Mo	F5
Tribune (rue de la)	B	K5
Trinité (parvis de la)	XL	J11
Triomphe (bld. du)	Au	O11-P12
Trois Ponts (rue des)	Au	PQ12
Trône (place du)	B	J7
Trône (rue du)	B-XL	K8-L9
‘t Serclaes (rue)	B	I6
Tuinbouw	Ev	Q2
Tulipe (rue de la)	XL	K8-9
Tulipier (rue du)	Fo	E12

● U ●

Ulens (rue)	Mo	G2-H3
Une Personne (rue d’)	B	I6
Union (rue de l’)	SJ	K4-5
Ursulines (rue des)	B	H7
Uytroever (rue M.)	Ko	C1

● V ●

Vaes (rue)	Fo	E10
Vaillance (pl. de la)	An	B8
Valduc (rue)	Au	QR12
Valkeners (av. Alph.)	Au	QR11
Vallée (rue de la)	B-XL	K11
Vallon (rue du)	SJ	L5
Van Aa (rue)	XL	KL9
Van Artevelde (rue)	B	G6
Van Beesen (avenue)	JP	E1

STREETS	PARISH COUNCILS	PLAN
Van Bemmel (rue)	SJ	L5
Van Boterdael (rue J.)	An	A7
Van Bergen (rue)	Ko	EF2
Van Campenhout (rue)	B	N5-6
Van Caulaert (sq. Gr.)	SG	F10
Van Cauwenbergh (rue E.)	Mo	FG1
Van den Berghe (r. G.)	An	AB8
Vandenboogaerde (r.)	Mo	G2
Vandenbranden (rue)	B	G5
Vandenbroeck (rue)	XL	L9
Vandenbussche (rue)	Sc	N3
Van Den Corput (rue)	Fo	G12
Vandendriessche (avenue Roger)	WP	R9
Vandenpeereboom (rue A.)	Mo	D4-5
Vanderborght (rue P.)	JP-Ko	DE1
Van Der Bruggen (avenue Raymond)	An	C8
Van Der Bruggen (square E.)	An	BC8
Van Der Dussen (rue)	Mo	E4
Van Der Elst (rue)	B	I4-5
Vanderhaegen (rue)	B	GH8
Vanderhoeft (r. Vict.)	Sc	O1-2
Vanderhoeven (rue)	SJ	M5
Vanderkindere (r. A.)	Mo	E5
Vanderlinden (rue)	Sc	K1
Vandermaelen (rue)	Mo	G4
Vandermeeren (rue)	An-Mo	D6
Vandermeersch (rue)	Sc	K2
Van Der Meulen (rue)	B	J5
Van der Noot (rue)	Mo	F2
Vanderperren (rue)	JP	F1
Vanderschrick (rue)	SG	G9-10
Vandersmissen (r. J.)	Et-WP	Q10
Vanderstappen (r. Ch.)	Sc	O1
Van Der Stichelen (rue)	Mo	G2
Vanderstraeten (rue)	Mo	EF5
Vandervelde (pl. Em.)	B	G7
Vandervelde (sq. Em.)	An	C8
Vander Weyden (r. R.)	B	H7
Vande Sande (r. Félix)	Ko	E2
Vande Sande (sq. Félix)	Ko	E2

STREETS	PARISH COUNCILS	PLAN
Vandevoorde (rue P.)	An	A8
Van De Weyer (rue)	Sc	KL2
Van Driessche (r. Em.)	XL	I12
Van Dyck (rue Rom.)	An	A6
Van Dyck (rue)	Sc	KL3
Van Elewijck (rue)	XL	K10
Van Eyck (rue)	B-XL	K12
Van Gaver (rue)	B	H4
Van Gele (rue Colonel)	Et	NO9
Van Haelen (bld.Guill.)	Fo	EF11-12
Van Hamme (rue)	Sc	M4
Van Hasselt (rue A.)	Sc-SJ	M4
Van Helmont (rue)	B	H6-7
Van Hemelrijk (rue T.)	Mo	A4
Van Hoegaerde (place)	Ko-Mo	F3
Van Hoegaerde (rue)	Ko-Mo	F3
Van Hoorde (rue)	Sc	L3
Van Hove (rue)	Sc	L4
Van Huffel (pl. H)	Ko	EF3
Van Humbeek (rue P.)	Mo	D5
Van Kalck (rue)	Mo	BC4
Van Laethem (rue G.)	Ev	R3
Van Lier (r. Martin)	An	A8
Van Lierde (r. Jean)	An	A6
Van Lint (rue)	An	E7-8
Van Maerlant (rue)	B	LM7
Van Malder (rue)	Mo	E4-5
Van Male de Ghorain (rue)	Mo	F4
Van Meenen (pl. M.)	SG	GH11
Van Meyel (place)	Et	N8
Van Meyel (rue)	Mo	GH2
Van Moer (rue)	B	I8
Vanne (rue de la)	B-XL	J10
Van Orley (rue)	B	K5
Van Ostade (rue)	B	O6-7
Van Overbeke (av.)	Ga	C1
Van Praet (rue Jules)	B	H6
Van Ruusbroeck (r. J.)	Ev	P1
Van Schoor (rue)	Sc	K1
Van Soust (rue)	An	ABC6
Van Vollenhoven (av. Ambassadeur)	Sc	M2
Van Volsem (r. Jean)	XL	L9-K10
Van Volxem (avenue)	Fo	D12-E10-11
Van Wambeke (rue)	An	A5-6
Van Ysendyck (rue)	Sc	M1
Van Zande (rue A.)	BA-Mo	B2
Vauthier (rue)	B-XL	L8
Vautour (rue du)	B	G6
V-Day (av. du)	Ev	R4
Venise (rue de)	XL	K9-10
Verbiest (rue Jean)	Mo	AB3
Verbist (rue)	Sc-SJ	M5
Verboeckhaven (rue)	Sc-SJ	L4
Verdonck (rue D.)	An	C6
Verdure (rue de la)	B	G6
Vergnies (rue de)	XL	K10
Vergote (rue)	Sc	P6
Vergote (square)	Sc-WL	P6
Verhaegen (rue Théod.)	SG	FG10
Verhaeren (sq. Albert)	XL	M11
Verhas (rue)	Sc	L1
Verheggen (rue Eug.)	Fo-SG	G12
Verheyden (rue)	An-Mo	CD6
Verheyden (rue Is.)	XL	J9
Vérité (rue de la)	An	B7-8
Vermicellerie (r. de la)	Mo	F3
Véronèse (rue)	B	N6
Verrept-Dekeyser (rue)	Mo	F5
Verriest (rue H.)	Ev	R3-4
Verstraeten (r. Liévin)	Au	P12
Verte (rue)	Sc-SJ	J3-K2-3
Verveine (rue de la)	B	M7
Verviers (rue de)	B-SJ	L6
Verwée (rue)	Sc	L1
Vésale (rue)	B	J5
Vétérans Coloniaux (square des)	An	C7
Vétérinaires (rue des)	An-SG	DE9
Veydt (rue)	SG	IJ10
Viaduc (rue du)	XL	KL9
Victoire (rue de la)	SG	H9-10-I10-11
Victoria Regina (av.)	B	JK4
Victoria Regina (sq.)	SJ	J4
Vieillards (rue des)	SG	G10
Vieille-Halle-aux-Blés	B	I6
Vierge Noire (rue de la)	B	H5

STREETS	PARISH COUNCILS	PLAN
Vierges (rue des)	B	G6
Vieujant (rue Jules)	Mo	D4
Vieux-Marché-aux-Grains (rue du)	B	H5
Vifquin (rue)	Sc	L2-3
Vilain XIV (rue)	B-XL	K11
Village (rue du)	An	B8
Villa Hermosa (rue)	B	J7
Villard (rue H.)	Sc	M3
Villas (avenue des)	Fo-SG	G11
Villers (rue des)	B	H7
Vincotte (rue Thomas)	Sc	M4-5
Vindictive (rue du)	Et	O9
Violette (pet. r. de la)	B	I6
Violette (rue de la)	B	I6
Visitandines (rue des)	B	H7
Vivier (rue du)	XL	M9
Vleurgat (ch. de)	B-XL	K11-12
Vlogaert (rue)	SG	G9
Vogler (rue)	Sc	L1-2
Voirie (quai de la)	B2	H3
Volders (av. Jean)	SGG	9
Volontaires (av. des)	Au-Et-WP	P11-Q10
Voltaire (avenue)	Sc	M1-2
Vonck (rue)	Sc-SJ	L4
Vondel (rue)	Sc	KL1

• W •

STREETS	PARISH COUNCILS	PLAN
Wafelaerts (rue Henri)	SG	H12
Wahis (bld. Gnral)	Sc	O3-4
Wallons (place des)	B	H7
Walschaerts (rue Egide)	SG	F10-11
Wangermée (rue Gén.)	Et	O9
Wappers (place)	B-Sc	O6
Wappers (rue)	B	O6
Washington (rue)	XL	J11-12
Waterloo (bld. de)	B	IJ8
Waterloo (ch. de)	SG-XL	H11-I-J12
Waterloo (gal. de)	XL	J12
Waterloo Wilson (r. J.)	B	M5-6
Watteeu (rue)	B	I7-8
Wauters (rue Joseph)	Sc	O1
Wauters-Koeckx (pl.)	Mo	F3-4
Wauters-Koeckx (rue)	Mo	F4
Wauwermans (rue)	SJ	M5
Wavre (chaussée de)	Au-Et-XL	JKL8-MN9-OP10-11-QR12
Wayenberg (rue)	XL	L9
Wayez (rue)	An	BC8
Werrie (pl. Philippe)	JP	F1
Wéry (rue)	XL	L9-10
Wielemans-Ceuppens (avenue)	Fo	EF11
Wielemans-Ceuppens (place)	Fo	DE11
Wiertz (rue)	B-XL	L8
Willebroeck (quai de)	B2	HI2-3
Willems (rue)	SJ	L5
Willemyns (rue A.)	An	A8
Wilmotte (rue Maurice)	SG	HI11
Winteroy (rue)	BA	A1
Wittmann (rue Em.)	Sc	NO4
Woeringen (rue de)	B	G7
Woeste (av. Charles)	JP	F1
Wolles (rue Camille)	Sc	P3
Woluwe St.-Lambert (avenue de)	WL	Q8-R7
Wytsman (rue Juliette)	XL	M11-12

• Y •

STREETS	PARISH COUNCILS	PLAN
Ypres (bld. d')	B	H3-4
Yser (avenue de l')	Et	O7
Yser (place de l')	B	H3

• Z •

STREETS	PARISH COUNCILS	PLAN
Zéphir (rue du)	WL	R6
Zinner (rue)	B	K6
Zwaab (rue Michel)	Mo	FG2